MEDITATION
WITHOUT
MYTH·

MEDITATION

WITHOUT

MYTH

What I Wish They'd Taught Me in Church
about Prayer, Meditation, and
the Quest for Peace

Daniel A. Helminiak

A Crossroad Book
Crossroad Publishing Company
New York

The Crossroad Publishing Company
481 Eighth Avenue, Suite 1550, New York, NY 10001

This book is set in 11/14 Minion.
The display type is Keeple.

Printed in the United States of America

Library of Congress Cataloging-in-Publication Data

Helminiak, Daniel A.
    Meditation without myth : what I wish they'd taught me in church
about prayer, meditation, and the quest for peace / Daniel A. Helminiak.
        p. cm.
    Includes bibliographical references.
    ISBN 0-8245-2308-3 (alk. paper)
    1. Meditation. 2. Humanism, Religious. 3. Meditation—Christianity.
I. Title.
BL627.H42 2005
204'.35—dc22

                                                    2005009451

1   2   3   4   5   6   7   8   9   10   09   08   07   06   05

To Raymond Machesney
dear and loyal lifelong friend
rare philosophical soul mate
golden human being

In memory of
Larry Alan Miller

Contents

Preface

The times are in turmoil. Culture wars rage. At stake are spiritual matters—the beliefs and values that structure people's lives.

Historians tell us that, in periods of social unrest, opposing trends tend to emerge. A conservative political force tries to shore up the status quo, to hold back change, to stop the dizzying spin of novelty. The fundamentalism of our age exemplifies this trend. On the other hand, creative interest in spirituality also mushrooms. People question their beliefs. They rethink their values. They explore new religions, study arcane metaphysical systems, and engage in varied spiritual practices. People dig deep into themselves and into life to try and find new meaning, new purpose, a new vision of things.

My emphasis has been the spiritual—not because of my recent role in the current culture wars, but because of a natural propensity with which I grew up and because of my early commitment to a vocation in the Catholic priesthood. As a theologian and a psychology professor—with a Ph.D. in each field—as well as a sincere seeker, over the years I did considerable work to understand and grow in the spiritual life. Now my personal quest is dovetailing with the historical trend, and I am in a position to make some possible contribution. By sharing my spiritual insight, I might serve as a guide to others whom the changing times have forced onto the spiritual path.

With this book I make my offering. In three prior books I treated this material in extensive technical detail: *Spiritual Development: An Interdisciplinary Study* (Loyola University Press, 1987), *The Human Core of Spirituality: Mind as Psyche and Spirit* (State University of New York Press, 1996), and *Religion and the Human Sciences: An Approach via Spirituality* (State University of New York Press, 1998). Here I make a popular presentation that speaks to a broad audience.

Oftentimes more a psychologist than a theologian, I focus on the inner human workings of meditation and spiritual growth. My uncommon goal is to forge a true science of spirituality. Yet I couch this analysis in a broader context that includes belief in God and the practice of religion. This thoroughly humanistic analysis with a natural opening to theology is, I believe, unique. The emphasis within Buddhism is the closest parallel, yet Buddhism has no concern for the questions about God that characterize Western religions. And Western approaches to this topic tend to focus on the divine, rather than the human, and, indeed, often identify the two. I cleanly sort out the psychological and the theological and then interrelate them. In the process I apply the best of contemporary psychology and invoke the teachings of mystics throughout the ages. I know of no other approach that maintains this delicate balance.

My focus is our common humanity and its spiritual core. My vision is a global community. Thus, I address spiritual seekers of all religions and denominations, and not only religious folk but also the spiritually sensitive who have no interest in organized religion. What I present is the spiritual dimension of the human experience itself, so my emphasis relates to the daunting challenge presented by a globalizing world of pluralism and diversity in the twenty-first century. Indeed, as the religious traditions have always held, profound spirituality taps into an underground stream that links the whole human race and flows into a pervasive transcendent reality. With this book I want to help people connect with all humanity and touch that reality.

I first presented this material for a silent meditation retreat in January, 2002. I am grateful to Gay Spirit Visions of Atlanta, and especially King Thackston (R.I.P.), for the invitation to lead that retreat. The topic of meditation proved exceedingly useful. Although a practical matter, something to be done, meditation opens onto most of the psychological and theological issues at stake in the spiritual life. So the focus on meditation allows this book to address essential spiritual issues in a concrete manner.

I am also grateful to John Jones and The Crossroad Publishing Company for their commitment to this book. And I thank so many others who helped with this project. My beloved colleague from the University of West Georgia, Professor Emeritus Anne Richards, provided me her customary extensive criticism of an early draft of this work. Others also provided similar feedback, encouragement, and support: Elliot Altschal, Kerry Clark, Geoff Corbin, Richard Hardy, Allan Helminiak, Raymond Machesney, Dick Marshall, Cecelia McHirella, Rob McHirella, Robert Pozzi, and Peter VanDenEng. For the support of family and friends, which allows me to pursue my esoteric, solitary work, I am most grateful. Of course, I must take full responsibility for what I have written here. It is not to be assumed that these others fully agree with my position.

Finally, I am grateful to you, my dear readers, for your willingness to attend to my words and thoughts. May this book be of benefit to you. Together, grounded in what is most noble and worthy in the human soul, may we find a common vision to sustain us and our world.

PART ONE

Taming the Mind

CHAPTER I

In Quest of Spiritual Understanding

W HEN I WAS YOUNGER, I wanted to be a saint. A well-behaved child, I did what I was told, and even more. I worked to be the best at everything. In the Polish Catholic community in Pittsburgh where I grew up, the best one could be was a priest, and the best priest was a holy one. So, at an immature seventeen, I entered a Catholic seminary. I was ordained, served in a parish, and then pursued an educational ministry. I later left the priesthood to work full-time as a psychology professor and lecturer. According to official Catholic teaching, while in my soul I am a priest forever, I have betrayed God and the Church in taking up my own life; and I am a sinner, hardly a saint. This judgment does not matter to me now. My understanding of sanctity has changed. The same forces that led me into the seminary to be a saintly priest continue to guide my life. But these days I just try to be a good person—honest, just, loving, compassionate.

In seminary I diligently followed all the rules. I was one of the few who actually attempted to use those early morning periods set aside for personal prayer in chapel after Mass. I knelt up straight, fought sleep, and day after day struggled to meditate.

Every Wednesday evening after dinner and recreation period during my latter college years, we had a "spiritual conference" in the basilica crypt. That space lent itself to spiritual pursuits—

deep, dark, mysterious; punctuated with short, fat columns; covered with a vaulted ceiling; lined by alcoves enclosing private altars. As I remember it, the monk assigned as spiritual director gave the same talk every week. He spoke of the need to build a solid foundation: a house built on sand could not long stand. I certainly wanted to build such a foundation in my soul, and I kept wondering what it meant to build such a foundation. The practical meaning of that metaphor eluded me. I faithfully put in what efforts I could, but I saw no progress in my spiritual construction. I seemed to have no deeper goodwill or stronger virtue than I had had when I was living at home.

We had week-long, silent retreats every year. These were to be times of "intense spiritual pursuit." After a good retreat, we were supposed to be spiritually renewed, refreshed, strengthened, but after a week's retreat I was usually just tired of trying to be spiritual. I was happy to get back to a regular schedule of classes, recreation, and conversation at meals.

Week after week after those spiritual conferences, I would return to my room through the monastery corridors, processing with the other seminarians in our long, flowing, black cassocks, heads bowed, and silent. Week after week, I would think to myself, "Somebody must know something about this stuff!"

I do not believe that anybody really did at that time. Sometimes when I read student papers today, I come away wondering what the students were trying to say. Paragraph after paragraph the papers go on, using words that don't fit together and sentences that have no logical connections. The sentences make no sense because their authors don't know what the words mean. Although the grammar may be correct and the sentence structure standard, the result is gibberish.

I used to get that same impression from those weekly spiritual conferences. The monk used all the spiritual words, quoted all the relevant doctrines, faithfully supported the official Catholic teaching, and even quoted Jesus from time to time, but on the whole made no sense. In Rome as a seminarian, I learned an Italian word for such talks: *fervorino*—an inspirational, exhortatory sermon. The talk was supposed to motivate you. But motivate you for what? What was the task we were to pursue? Despite all the goodwill in the world, I didn't know how to direct my efforts.

Similarly, I did not know how to make use of those long, silent days of retreat or the "meditation period" after morning Mass. I did not know what I was supposed to be doing to "meditate." The bigger problem was that, as far as I could make out, nobody else did, either! Oh, there were inspirational books on prayer, meditation, and holiness, and I read them. There were meditation books to follow, the "daily thought" sort of thing, and I used them. There was even a required course on spiritual theology, and I poured over the dry and tedious text. My major impression remained: nobody knows what this stuff is about. Or in any case, I was not getting it.

I was not alone. A friend in New York City, also a former priest, recently started meditating at a Buddhist center. He was pleasantly surprised to learn how much the Buddhists know about the process of meditation. Referring to our seminary days, he stated outright, "Meditation time was for sleeping."

Only years later did I have any major insight into spirituality. By then I had been ordained seven years, had served four years as an associate pastor in a large suburban parish, had spent a year as a junior member on a seminary faculty, and was now pursuing doctoral studies in systematic theology. I had made some bumbling progress in my spiritual pursuits. In the most self-determined decision of my life thus far, I had left parish ministry to become involved in seminary education. I was beginning to find myself. By then, I had also abandoned slavish commitment to praying the breviary. I had definitely outgrown the annual priestly retreats. And I found the courage to do something about the situation. I began making my annual retreat at a Buddhist meditation center.

New Directions

In the Buddhist retreats I discovered many of the same elements that were part of my own spiritual tradition: silence through most of the day, performance of assigned menial tasks, abandonment of one's given name for a name that expressed one's new spiritual identity, the wearing of ritual garments, affiliation with a new community, and, above all, long periods of meditation. But the Buddhists had a genuine understanding of these things, and through the Buddhist perspective I began to recognize why these things were a part of my own haphazard spiritual formation, and I began to understand what psychological effects they were supposed to have. Most important of all, the Buddhists taught me how to use periods of silence to deprogram the crazy-making, repetitive thoughts that went round and round in my head and to open my mind to a realm of serene transcendence.

What most impressed me about the Buddhist approach is this: it had nothing to do with theology. Oh, Buddhism has its beliefs, just like any other religion, and oftentimes they are just as fanciful, but Buddhist teaching regarding meditation is supremely practical. It is based on centuries of attention to meditative practice and deals specifically with the workings of the mind. There is nothing in Buddhist teaching comparable to Christian "grace," the "gifts of the Holy Spirit," "acquired" and "infused contemplation," or reliance on the "supernatural" work of "God" in the "soul," the words I heard so much in my Catholic upbringing. Nor did the Buddhism I encountered make much ado about spiritual entities with extraordinary knowledge, out-of-body travel, and supposed metaphysical realms, about which many contemporary spiritual movements are concerned.

In Buddhist meditative practice, theology or metaphysics do not complicate the spiritual quest. There is no appeal to a magical mentality—the idea that somehow God grants spiritual insight to specially chosen souls or that we might be lucky enough to make contact with superior beings or that spiritual integration is purely a gift about which we can have no understanding. The Buddhist approach is wholly humanistic: it is based on the observable workings of the human mind. It proposes meditative techniques that address those workings in specific and specialized ways. It offers a method to tame the mind and to profit from long periods of silence.

Growing up in that Polish, mill-working community in Pittsburgh gave me more than a spiritual longing. It also gave me a strong dose of down-to-earth practicality. My practical bent was delighted to encounter the Buddhist approach to spirituality. Now I could go about my pursuit of holiness in a systematic way.

Meditation without Myth

Such a humanistic approach to spirituality is what I present in this book—not a specifically Buddhist approach, but a generic humanistic approach to which my Buddhist experience tipped me off. I want to present what I have discovered as the human core of all spirituality. I want to talk of spirituality without involving God or other supposed spiritual entities and realms. The psychological advances of the last few decades now make it possible to some extent to explain spiritual development scientifically. Spiritual advancement is not specifically a matter of God's grace or divine intervention or metaphysical speculation or cosmic forces. It is simply a matter of good psychology and honest living.

My title *Meditation without Myth* suggests this humanistic emphasis. I want to explain how meditation works. I want to take the magic or myth out of concern for spirituality. In doing so, I do not intend to get rid of God or religious belief and practice. I simply want to clarify how religion fits with what we now know of spiritual psychology. The two can fit together. But to fit psychology and religion together, we need first to tease them apart. And most of all, we need to propose a truly psychological explanation of spiritual growth—one that could stand on its own for nonreligious people and, for religious people, could honestly fit with authentic religion.

Is it even possible to approach spirituality in so secular a way? How could we explain spiritual growth without involving God? Isn't the spiritual realm precisely the realm of God and religion?

These questions are completely understandable; they express legitimate concerns. In fact, they arise because—as I have been saying—there is precious little understanding available regarding spiritual growth. Despite the mushrooming of interest in recent decades, when it comes to spirituality most people are still where I was, along with my fellow seminarians, the monks, and the staff, when I was in seminary. Spirituality is still a realm full of esoteric claims, metaphysical speculation, imagined powers and entities, fanciful promises, and fuzzy thinking. With this book I propose to bring some clarity to the matter.

Is such an achievement even possible? You, dear reader, will have to judge for yourself after reading this book. Surely, I cannot say in one easy paragraph what I took a book to write. But let me begin by drawing a comparison with another quest for understanding.

Isaac Newton is famous for his explanation of the solar system. In fact, Newton was an extremely devout Christian. He believed that he was explaining God's creation. In his mind, he had figured out the mathematical marvels that God built into the solar system. But Newton did not include "God" in his mathematical equations. Naming God would not have helped one bit. As Newton knew well, his equations regarded God's handiwork. The physical universe is what concerned Newton, not God. God was outside of—God was beyond—the matter to be explained, so God had no place in Newton's mathematical formulas.

Similarly, we can believe that God is at work in our spiritual growth—just as God is somehow behind the solar system and behind all reality. But even as in the seventeenth century Newton was able to explain certain aspects of the physical universe, we are at a point in history when we can begin to explain spiritual phenomena. On the basis of the workings of the human mind, we can propose a scientific understanding of the spiritual quest. God, grace, the Holy Spirit, or other supposed spiritual entities do not belong in a scientific explanation of spiritual growth. Mixing God up in the matter—like quoting the Bible to explain nuclear energy—can actually mislead us, distract us, and confuse our spiritual quest. So I propose a wholly humanistic understanding of spirituality.

Nonetheless, for those who wish, I will bring God back into the picture later in this book. Understandably, for many people discussion of God is essential, so discussion of God will be of supreme importance for this book. But in the meantime, on the basis of psychological analyses and apart from theology or religion, I proceed to explain spirituality as a purely human phenomenon.

In the first part of this book, I will get down to brass tacks and explain how one does meditation. In the second part, I will apply contemporary psychology to explain why meditative practice works. Finally, in the third part, I will explain what this practice has to do with God, ethics, spiritual experiences, and good living in general.

I intend to present spirituality as a natural aspect of the human mind, something fully open to religious believers and nonbelievers alike, indeed, something required by our human constitution and the human condition itself. Thus, I present an account of spirituality that should be supremely useful in the secularized world of competing religions, cultures, and markets. I offer a vision and practical spiritual advice for sane living in a pluralistic world. In short, I share the understanding of spirituality that I wish had been available to me during my own seminary training.

CHAPTER 2

The Human as Body, Psyche, and Spirit

O RDAINED A CATHOLIC PRIEST, I was on a spiritual quest. Inevitably, my quest led me to search beyond my own Catholic tradition. I began doing retreats at a Buddhist meditation center. I learned how to meditate and began to understand how meditation works. Rather than focusing on God, Buddhism focuses on the human mind. Within the mind there is a self-transcending dimension that specific meditation practices can unleash. The Buddhists speak of this dimension as "Buddha Nature." This idea was already familiar to me, though the terminology was different. Western philosophy regularly refers to a spiritual dimension in humanity. Even in popular circles, talk of "the human spirit" is commonplace. Could it be that attention to the human spirit, and not God or religion, is the key to spiritual growth? The Buddhists certainly thought so, and my own philosophical, theological, and psychological training led me to agree.

In this chapter, I will briefly summarize this nontheological understanding of spiritual growth. Part 2 presents it in much more detail. Here I want only to introduce, not fully explain, these fascinating ideas about body, psyche, and spirit because I want to use them to get down to brass tacks and examine the different kinds of spiritual practices. The details will become clearer as this book unfolds.

Spirituality apart from Theology

My experience with Buddhist meditation was a major break-through. It led me to understand meditation on the basis of the human mind itself. Through my study of humanistic psychology, I made another important connection. I found a link between Eastern and Western thought. I realized that the "human potential," about which Abraham Maslow, Carl Rogers, Rollo May, and other humanistic and existentialist psychologists speak, was more or less the same self-transcending dimension of the human mind that Buddhism emphasizes.

Unlike most other approaches, humanistic psychology is concerned with human health and growth, not human pathology—and human advance and achievement, not mere mediocre adjustment. Humanistic psychology highlights a dimension of our mental experience that leads us ever beyond our upbringing, our culture, and our own selves. Too often we live our lives from behind a protective screen. We shield ourselves by unconsciously using what Freud called defense mechanisms—such as denial, repression, rationalization, projection, and reaction formation. But freed from the distortions that our defense mechanisms impose, this growth-oriented dimension of the mind releases deep and rich inner experience, childlike delight in living, genuine concern for others, creativity in daily activities, and extraordinary personal uniqueness. In all these effects, about which humanistic psychology speaks, I was again hearing echoes of spirituality.

Most important of all, during the years when I was making Buddhist retreats, in my doctoral theology program I was studying under Bernard Lonergan. He was a Canadian Jesuit philosopher, theologian, and methodologist, said to be one of the geniuses of the twentieth century. His main works are *Insight: A Study of Human Understanding* and *Method in Theology*. As the very titles of his books suggest, his focus was the human mind and its application to the range of human activities—intellectual, artistic, mystical, commonsensical, theoretical. Building on Plato, Aristotle, Augustine, Aquinas, Galileo, Kant, Hegel, Einstein, Heisenberg, Gödel, and other giants of Western civilization, Lonergan proposed an analysis of human consciousness.

> The human spirit seems to open onto the divine,
> onto what is all-pervasive, lasting, true, and good.
> No wonder that the spiritual is so easily
> confused with the divine!

In several places in his writings, Lonergan uses the word *spirit* in place of consciousness. I took this indication seriously, and I took Lonergan's writings to be a highly elaborated account of the structures and workings of the human spirit. Applying this account to what I knew of spirituality, I found that I could make sense of most of what people say about spirituality without needing to get into theology or esoteric metaphysics. I was able to propose a coherent psychology of spirituality. I could offer an account of spiritual growth based on the nature of the human mind.

Thus, from a number of different sources—Buddhist psychology, Western talk of the human spirit, humanistic psychology, and Lonergan's profound analyses of human consciousness—pieces came together. I had come upon a basis for an understanding of spiritual growth apart from all religion and theology.

The key to this understanding is the human spirit. What exactly is it?

Spirit

The human spirit is a dimension of mental experience that you can recognize in your own self. Most fundamentally, it manifests itself in our spontaneous sense of wonder, marvel, and awe. Whenever we stop in our tracks and say, "Wow, what was that?" or "How peculiar!" or "Totally awesome!" or "Yes, I get it!"—our spirit has been activated. It is taking us out of ourselves. It is broadening our experience. It is opening us to a bigger reality. It is moving us beyond the here and now. It is leading us to transcend our former state. It is pointing us toward personal growth.

How far can the human spirit take us? It is geared toward everything. It is the basis of our every conscious experience, and the human spirit is open-ended in its reach. It expresses itself in awareness that unfolds onto unlimited vistas. It expresses itself in a never-ending flow of questions, which seek an ever-expanding range of understanding. It expresses itself in choices and decisions as it reaches out in love to identify with all that is good and beautiful. In the ideal, it would become one with all that is. In its reach for what is true and good, it goes beyond the here and now and beyond the this and that. It points to what pertains everywhere and always, to what pervades and holds together an array of particular things, to what is lasting, to what could be called eternal. The reach of the human spirit is potentially unbounded.

Thus, the spirit is a dimension of our own minds that takes us beyond the merely physical world. Through everyday ordinary things like ideas and ideals, the human spirit opens us to a transcendent realm of experience. Indeed, at its farthest reach the human spirit seems to open onto the divine, onto what is all-pervasive, lasting, true, and good. No wonder that the spiritual is so easily confused with the divine! Yet what I am describing here is a part of our own selves. This growing openness to all reality in marvel and awe is a dimension of everyday experience. This wondrous experience is the result of the human spirit: this experience is spiritual. If this talk of the wonder of your own mind fascinates you, you are even now experiencing your spiritual nature.

Psyche

Still, the human spirit is not the sole facet of the human mind. We next look at psyche. Within human mental experience there are also emotions, memories, and images, and these all come together to structure personality. I do not use "personality" in the popular sense to indicate someone who is attractive and congenial—"She really has personality!"—but in the psychological sense in which everyone, whatever his or her personal style, has a personality. In this sense personality is simply a particular manner of being a person. "Personality" is a sum total of habitual patterns of responding. The fact that some of us are outgoing and others more reserved, some are taken up with big ideas and others attend to details—these are matters of different personalities. The differences are structured into people's minds.

Following Lonergan, I call this second set of mental structures *psyche*, and it is what psychologists most often deal with in the counseling office. In comparison with the human spirit, psyche is a more stable aspect of the mind. Whereas the spirit wants to break out and transcend to new spaces, the psyche finds contentment in a stable status quo. Thus, the human spirit is not completely free to soar in its open-ended quest, for it is "housed" in psychic structures. Thus, the psyche is both a boon and a bane to the spirit. The psyche both supports and restricts the spirit.

Psyche affects spirit. When anxiety colors a person's mental life, the likelihood of striking out on a new adventure is slight, so one's life remains dull and humdrum, locked in confining routines, and there is no growth. When overenthusiasm habitually pushes a person to faulty judgments and rash decisions, the possibilities for solid and steady personal growth likewise fall by the wayside. On the other hand, when appropriate images readily come to mind to suggest the solution to a problem and when emotions contribute supportively as a person thinks the problem through, penetrating insight, reasonable judgment, and reliable progress easily ensue. In sum, when the workings of psyche are securely in place, the spirit is free to soar; but when psyche is a cauldron of chaos, emotional ups and downs, the human spirit is also embroiled, struggling for mere survival.

Conversely, spirit can also affect psyche. We can decide to break a bad habit. We can develop a sense of humor. We can learn to be more open-minded. We can recognize our blind spots and start acting more fairly. That is to say, with a deliberate effort we can restructure our personalities. We can change the spontaneous reactions that make us the kind of person we are.

For good or ill, psyche and spirit work together in the human mind. For this reason careful attention to emotions, interpersonal relationships, and lifestyle is a prerequisite of any serious spiritual pursuit. Without deliberate work on personal growth, we cannot be spiritually awake. Talking about a middle-aged acquaintance of his whose life was dead-ending, my brother once made a comment that hits this nail on the head: "This guy just never made the effort to develop his character."

Ah, now these things begin to make some sense! During my seminary training, there was this constant push to overcome your sins and imperfections. That emphasis seemed so negative. It made me uptight and guilt-ridden. Now I see that behind that emphasis was a clumsy attempt to foster personal growth. Unfortunately, the personal growth got lost in a cloud of guilt, sin, and neurotic self-consciousness. The focus on sin and repentance shut us down instead of opening us up. Talk of pleasing God and keeping the commandments distracted attention from the real issues: bad habits and wrongful behaviors do not hurt God as much as they hurt us. They narrow our perspective; they shrink our horizon; they keep us from growing. The textbooks called the first stage of the spiritual life the "purgative stage." It was the effort to clean up one's act, to "purge" oneself of negative qualities. Understood psychologically, not moralistically, this purgative stage makes so much more sense. This is not to say that we don't sometimes deliberately do wrong; we do sin. But most people really are good-willed; most try to be good people. For the most part, our problem is not ill will. Our problem is bad habits and counterproductive reactions that somehow got built into us as we were growing up. The purgation that is needed is to drop our defensiveness and to open up more fully to life.

So the mind is psyche and spirit, and the two work together. Because these two elements tug at us inside our own minds, we can get stuck in a neurotic rut, or we can unleash our unlimited potential. This process of unleashing our built-in potential is the essence of spiritual growth.

Body

However, the human being is not just a mind, not just psyche and spirit. We are also animals. We have physical bodies. We are biological organisms. In addition to our psyches, our biology also influences the functioning of our human spirits. Indeed, our psyches and our spirits arise out of the marvel of human biology. So physical needs, drives, tendencies, urges, and sensitivities also color our mental life. When we are sick or weary, we cannot even think straight. The state of our bodies affects the state of our minds. When we are well rested, nourished, and exercised, our minds function more effectively; we tend to be upbeat, alert, and engaged; and our spirits, too, are alive: a sound mind in a sound body. Thus, a third factor makes up a human being: the body—or, more accurately, the organism, for the body in question is not just a physical body but also a living body.

Three facets, dimensions, factors, or aspects make up the human being: body, psyche, and spirit. I insist on these three, but the more standard ways of portraying the human being are different. Other approaches note only two facets. In the social sciences the human being is body and mind. In religious circles the human being is body and soul. The difference between mind and soul is not worth discussing here; it is a matter of mere shifting definition. The point is that both the social sciences and religion think of the human being as having two parts. In contrast, with Lonergan—and Buddhism—I understand the human being to be body, psyche, and spirit.

Lonergan suggests that talk simply of the "mind" or "soul" is seriously imprecise. Mind or soul refers to our inner life. But this inner life is complex; it includes at least two different dimensions: psyche and spirit. So the two-part, or bipartite, model of the human—body and mind or body and soul—needs to give way to a three-part, or tripartite, model—body, psyche, and spirit. Once this clarification is made, once the human mind is recognized as in part spiritual, we can begin to explain spirituality on the basis of the human mind itself. We do not have to appeal to God or to other metaphysical entities.

Other Models

Of course, not everybody thinks of the human being as simply body and soul or body and mind. We now hear of many multifaceted models of the human being. The list of supposed facets of the human being can be long: body, mind, soul, heart, psyche, consciousness, spirit, and the suggestions go on. But anything beyond body in those lists tends to be fuzzy and speculative. Still, these suggestions are worth thinking about. What we understand a person to be says a lot about how we will understand the spiritual quest. Consider a couple of other models of the human being.

A very popular model portrays the human as body, mind, and spirit. To some extent, this model appears to be an alternative to my own: body, psyche, and spirit; but I am wary of this popular model. In my understanding, spirit is an aspect of the inner life of a person, a part of the human mind, not something in addition to it. I am not sure what "spirit" means in the combination of body, mind, and spirit. "Mind" and "spirit" could mean many different things. This ambiguity is precisely the problem. I suspect that in this popular model "mind" refers to our inner life and "spirit" is added on to leave room for religion and concern about God. Today we are commonly aware that one's spirituality—and in this case the word is sometimes just a politically correct term for religion—is important to one's overall well-being. For example, all hospitals, whether religiously affiliated or not, are now required to provide some kind of "spiritual care." They usually do so by making a religious chaplain available to patients. So to allow for religion in a generic form, "spirit" is added to body and mind, and the suggestion is that, in addition to body and mind, a relationship with God or with some other nonhuman entity is essential to being a human being. But for this very reason, I am wary of this popular model. I think it suggests that spirituality depends on something external to the person, and that something, named or not, is God or some other supposed metaphysical entity. I recognize spirit, along with psyche, as a dimension of the human mind itself.

Yet another quite popular, current model of the human

being is right on target. This model includes three aspects: physical, emotional, and spiritual. This model is a close parallel to my own. This popular model is simple, easily understood, and accurate enough for many practical purposes. Instead of listing psyche or psychic—terms that might seem obscure—this model lists the "emotional." Most people understand what *emotional* means, and emotions are a key aspect of the psyche. So, without getting too technical, the "emotional" covers much the same ground as does the "psychic." Then the third element, the "spiritual," easily appears to be another inherent aspect of the human mind. When we talk of the "physical, emotional, and spiritual," the spiritual does not seem to be some external thing. Thus, the combination of physical, emotional, and spiritual presents a relatively accurate and very useful formula.

My sense is that body, psyche, and spirit—or more popularly: the physical, emotional, and spiritual—is the correct model. These three elements actually cover the field; they say completely what a human being is. Understood in Lonergan's sense, they are the necessary and sufficient to explain humanity; they are the elements in a scientific account of the human being. In any case, I take this understanding for granted in all that I present here.

One facet of the human being is spirit, and it provides a basis for talk of spirituality. Spiritual growth appears to be nothing other than the ever-further integration of the human spiritual capacity into the habitual functioning of the human being. Even granted that God set up this integrative, human process and is somehow behind it and is even the goal toward which it moves, bringing God into the discussion only complicates and confuses the matter at this point. Within a tripartite model of the human, careful attention to the human spirit already allows for a rich accounting of spirituality—as we will see below.

CHAPTER 3

Three Accesses to the Spirit

URING MY RELIGIOUS UPBRINGING and even through many years as a priest, I believed that a relationship with God was the key to spiritual growth. I imagined that because of my prayer and good living, God would grant me spiritual favors. I would become holy and, if very blessed, might even be given unusual gifts, such as visions, healings, and enraptured states of spiritual bliss. But despite my best efforts, none of these spiritual favors seemed to be coming to me. Besides, nobody I knew and nothing I read seemed to explain the spiritual life. Everything was a "mystery," and I was supposed to "take it on faith."

Over the years, my attempt to understand spiritual growth led me to this realization: the human spirit itself, not some other-worldly force, is the key to spiritual growth. The spirit is a dimension of our own human minds. To grow spiritually is to tap into it and unleash it. We become spiritual people by integrating our spiritual capacity more and more fully. So the task is not to prevail upon God to grant us spiritual favors. The task is to foster the working of our own spirit within us.

The practical question is this: How to engage the human spirit? There are three basic approaches: come in through the body, come in through the psyche, or go directly to the spirit.

Three facets constitute a human being: body, psyche, and spirit. And all three interact; they affect one another. Then there must be three accesses to the human spirit. Or, said otherwise, there are three ways to effect spiritual growth; there are three ways to enhance the spiritual within us; there are three ways to foster the ongoing integration of the spiritual into the permanent structures of the personality. First, you can emphasize the body or organism; second, you can focus on the psyche; or third, you can attend directly to the spirit. In each case, you can unleash the human spirit and foster spiritual integration. To explain what I mean, I will consider, in turn, the bodily, the psychic, and the spiritual (or direct) accesses to the human spirit.

The Body

First, spiritual practices that focus on the body are well known. Yoga is one of them. Through regulated breathing, stretching, and deliberate movements, yoga causes deep relaxation, clears the mind, and sometimes induces profound spiritual experiences. The matter is that simple.

Other bodily practices rely on specific nutritional regimens. Many people claim, for example, that vegetarianism is a spiritually useful practice. Fasting is another traditional spiritual practice that has its effect through the body. Fasting works by shifting body chemistry. Stop eating for a long while and you get light-headed; you begin to experience things differently. By fasting you induce an altered state of consciousness. Religions have generally considered such altered states to be spiritually useful: they open us to new perspectives.

A particularly striking, bodily spiritual practice is the sun dance of the Sioux and Cheyenne Indians. On skewers stuck through their pectoral muscles, young men hang themselves from a tall pole and remain exposed to the burning sun in a sacred ritual. Understandably, they often "psyche out," see "visions" (that is, hallucinate), and have "spiritual revelations."

These effects result from an assault to the body that, again, shifts body chemistry and, in particular, induces the release of endorphins, a brain chemical that produces a "high"—like what long-distance runners often experience. Similarly, members of religious orders in the West had a practice of self-flagellation: in the name of doing penance, they would whip themselves, often to the point of drawing blood. The mental effects are the same as in the Native American rituals.

Other spiritual practices in the West called for long hours of kneeling erect or praying with one's arms extended or interrupting deep sleep in the middle of the night (think of the Matins of Western monasticism, about which children sing in the ditty *Frère Jacques*). All these practices have known effects on the body and the mind, and all have been used to induce altered states of consciousness.

Less dramatically and more commonly, many religious rituals engage the body by requiring particular gestures and motions: kneeling, sitting, standing, bowing, spinning, prostrating oneself on the ground, folding one's hands, raising one's arms, holding hands with fellow congregants. These motions tend to ground one, to bring one back "down to earth," to restore one from one's mental wanderings to the here and now of one's body, and, when intense, to induce important changes in biological functioning. Thus, bodily actions affect the mind and open the possibility for a new perspective on things.

Again, the practice of hymn-singing, especially when all the verses are sung, affects the mind by requiring long periods of controlled, rhythmic breathing. And the ingestion of intoxicants, especially after a fast, also alters mental awareness. From a bio-psychological point of view, the wine that is a part of Christian communion is a strict parallel to the peyote of Native American rituals and the ayahuasca of Brazilian tribes. All are drugs that change mental functioning.

Religions have regularly employed bodily techniques to shift psychic balance. This shift, when done with understanding and goodwill, opens the mind to new spiritual sensitivity.

The Psyche

Second, other spiritual techniques focus specifically on the psyche. They have their effect by engaging the emotions and the imagination. Thus, for example, like good theater, any effective religious ritual should make one *feel* something: excitement, hope, sadness, loss, regret, anger, joy, resolve. Stirring the emotions shakes the structures of the psyche, looses encrusted patterns, and opens up new spiritual possibilities. For example, music is often a part of religious ritual. Music stirs the emotions. In addition, its rhythms—as also in drumming—have a profound effect on the brainstem and can induce a trancelike state, an altered state of consciousness. No wonder contemporary, modern dance music has a steady, pounding beat, and no wonder the pounding of jungle drums fascinates us.

Many common meditation techniques focus on the psyche. One such technique is to think about life and its meaning, and thus be moved to make positive resolutions. This approach is called discursive meditation. *Discursive* refers to thinking that moves from topic to topic and aims at rational analysis. We do discursive thinking when we are trying to solve a problem. Daily meditation books—such as Al-Anon's *Courage to Change* and so many others on the market today—propose inspiring topics for daily thought and guide one in pondering a worthy way of living. Such thinking and pondering is discursive meditation—prayerfully turning over a topic in one's mind. Many religions foster discursive meditation by encouraging reverent, daily reading of their sacred scriptures.

Beyond discursive thinking and sometimes as an aid to thinking, there are other powerful meditation techniques that engage the imagination. One common technique uses the imagination to conjure up some situation and put oneself in it. In the process, often unknown to the practitioner, subtle mental shifts occur, and after the meditation one finds oneself to be feeling and acting differently. Guided meditations work this way. You follow directions on an audiotape, often including relaxing music, or you follow the directions of a live guide or facilitator. At the same time you imagine yourself in quasi-mythical realms: wide open fields swaying with stalks of grain, bubbling brooks leading into the unknown, caverns burrowing deeply into massive mountains. In your mind you climb trees, explore forests, or float freely down flowing rivers. The images engage what Carl Jung called the "archetypes" of the unconscious, the deep and universal patterns that structure the human psyche. As you imagine yourself burrowing deeply into a cavern or hacking your way along a jungle path, you are "penetrating" into the secret spaces of your own unconscious. Thus, you make contact with long-forgotten emotional experiences or access hidden dreams; symbolically you bring them to the surface where you have a chance to deal with them. As a result, your outlook on life is purged of some defensiveness, and your spirit is more free to soar.

Such meditative practices access the power of imagery to dredge up the psyche and reconfigure it. These practices are among the most effective and readily available spiritual tools we have, and in one way or another they are built into all spiritual traditions. So powerful are these tools that their effects can be dramatic. These techniques should always be used with gentleness and care.

The Spirit

Third, there is a class of spiritual techniques that allow direct access to the spirit. These techniques bypass all thoughts, feelings, and images, putting them aside. Thus these techniques facilitate pure awareness. The goal is the experience of mere presence, just being there, without any distracting feelings, thoughts, or images—"distracting" because, at this point, attention to thinking, feeling, or imagining detours you from pure experience of the spirit. During this kind of meditation, the mind is perfectly calm. It is not busy with anything. It is operating on *no content*. It merely resides in a moment of total openness, experiencing, if anything, its own capacity for experience, its awareness of awareness.

Describing this meditative experience is difficult. Our language is designed for describing things in the physical world. It is made for talk of objects that stand in contrast to the experiencing subject: "I saw the car coming. The car skidded on the wet road." To some extent our language can also represent our inner experience: "I am glad there was no accident and nobody got hurt." Yet even here, our words still present an object—in this case, the feeling of gladness—as something we have, something other than ourselves, an object distinct from a subject. In the meditation I am describing here, however, you are not interested in any particular thing; you are not concerned with any object, whether external, like cars, roads, and wetness, or internal, like feelings, thoughts, and images. In this meditation, you are fully taken up with the experience of your own self as the experiencing subject. This experience is completely about subjectivity, not about objects. Our language is not well geared to deal with pure subjectivity, pure spirituality.

It is not necessary to describe this meditative state precisely. A story, however, may convey the idea of pure awareness. The story tells of a man who stopped at church late each afternoon on his way home from work. The local curate saw the man regularly and was puzzled by his action. The man would sit in the back pew, absolutely still and silent, looking straight ahead, and then, after a while, get up and leave. One day the curate approached the man and spoke inquiringly: "Tell me, sir, what do you do when you come here? You have no prayer book, Bible, or beads. Your lips do not move. You appear not to be praying. What do you do when you come here to church each day?"

The man replied simply: "It is always after a long and tiring day that I stop here to pray. So I just sit here and look at Him, and He just looks at me."

The man speaks of his silent and contentless communication with God. While this story is couched in religious terms, the style of his prayer perfectly illustrates the experience of pure spiritual presence. The man's mind is concerned with nothing—no words, no thoughts, no images, no feelings. He is simply yet actively present there. He sits at ease in a state of pure awareness.

My concern is not to remove God from the picture, but, on the contrary, to preserve some distinctive meaning for the term *God*.

Another example remains on a humanistic level. People in love often spend long hours together without any explicit communication. There comes a time in a relationship when all thoughts have been expressed, all feelings shared, and all words said. There is nothing more to do than simply be with each other—in delightful awareness of the beloved's presence with nothing more expected. Though probably more full of emotion that pure spiritual presence would be, this "merely-being-present" of lovers to one another is like pure spiritual presence. There is no content in the exchange. They are merely there with each other—though not passively present, but actively, alertly, engagingly so.

In fact, the mystics of the West often speak of their experience in terms of God's immediate presence to them or their immediate presence to God, so the analogy of lovers becomes very apropos. Small wonder that the standard mystical interpretation of the Bible's Canticle of Canticles or Song of Songs sees God and the "soul" as lovers in pursuit of each other.

True to the emphasis I have adopted here, however, I would rather speak of our absolute presence to being present, of our experience of our very capacity to experience, of our awareness of awareness itself. If others prefer to read God into this presence, this experience, this awareness, so be it. I see no need to make such a leap. Indeed, I see such a leap as unwarranted—unless we can specify what "God" and "presence to God" could possibly mean, beyond that to which I am referring, and specify why making a connection with God would be appropriate. My concern is not to remove God from the picture, but, on the contrary, to preserve some distinctive meaning for the term *God*. In the final analysis, if "God" is taken to be merely a name for the human experience of pure and open-ended awareness about which I am speaking, then we might conclude that there is no need to speak of God as a distinct reality in itself. Or else we might conclude that this humanistic approach is mistaken, since we are all actually God in our innermost core. In my mind, both conclusions would be misguided because each simplistically identifies the spiritual with the divine. In any case, I hope that those examples helped to suggest what is meant by the experience of pure presence beyond all thoughts, emotions, and images.

I have described how the body, psyche, and spirit can each be engaged to facilitate integration of the human spirit. What remains is to discuss in detail meditative techniques geared toward direct access to the spirit, and to introduce one technique at length. But first some further consideration of the human as body, psyche, and spirit is in order.

CHAPTER 4

Practical Implications of the Three-Part Model

⌇⌇⌇

FOR YEARS I HAVE BEEN on a quest to understand spiritual growth. A breakthrough came when I realized that the human being is body, psyche, and also spirit. With this realization I began to understand what spiritual practices are about: not about making contact with God, but accessing the human spirit. Since, as noted in chapter 3, the human is tripartite, there are three different accesses to the human spirit. This tripartite structure of the human has further implications. I will indicate three of them, after clarifying some terminology

Unfortunately, terminology from the East and the West referring to meditation can be very confusing, indeed contradictory. What the East calls contemplation, the West calls meditation, and vice versa. The Christian spiritual tradition understands meditation to refer to accesses via the psyche—the use of thought, emotion, and imagery. And contemplation refers to the absolutely quiet prayer of pure presence beyond all thought, feeling, and imagery. But for Eastern writers using English, contemplation usually refers to the process of thinking about something; contemplating means pondering or mulling over. And for Eastern writers meditation usually refers to spiritual practices that lead to a state of pure presence.

To avoid confusion, I will speak simply of different kinds of meditation. I propose the following terminology:

- *Discursive meditation* refers to the use of thought.
- *Affective meditation* refers to engaging the emotions.
- *Imageful meditation* refers to the use of imagination.
- *"Contentless" meditation* refers to techniques that facilitate states of pure presence beyond all thought, feeling, emotions, or images, beyond all mental content.

Since contentless meditation is the specific concern of this book, I will generally be referring to it when I say simply *meditation*, though I will be careful to specify my terms when confusion might occur.

There are three broad implications related to the fact that the human being is tripartite: body, psyche, and spirit.

People Are Different

First, despite the shared tripartite structure, people are different. Some are more comfortable with one or another of these facets of themselves. Some are gifted in one direction rather than another.

Consider the following example. On the basis of body structure, Sheldon developed a famous theory of personality types. He divided people into endomorphs, mesomorphs, and ectomorphs. Supposedly for completely normal and natural reasons, endomorphs express predominantly the inner layer of embryonic tissue from which fatty tissues and the internal organs—stomach, intestines, liver, kidneys—develop, so endomorphs tend to be plump, easygoing, and jovial; they also tend to be people-oriented. In contrast, mesomorphs express predominantly the middle layer of embryonic tissue from which the skeleton, muscles, and the circulatory system develop, so mesomorphs tend to be strong, well proportioned, and athletically gifted. Finally, ectomorphs express more the outer layer of embryonic tissue from which the skin, brain, and nervous system develop, so ectomorphs develop long and lanky bodies and tend to be "wiry," nervous types whose interests are artistic and scholarly. Whether this theory is valid or not—at the very least it oversimplifies—it illustrates that there are "different strokes for different folks." You probably recognize these three types among the people you know. Yet all people, despite their differences, develop from the same three embryonic layers, and, to some extent or other, all might possess interpersonal, athletic, and intellectual skills, though the emphases differ.

These questions should make it obvious that identifying inner experiences with the experience of God is problematic at best.

In some similar way, all people are body, psyche, and spirit. All function through all three facets of their makeup, yet propensities and emphases differ. As a result, different forms of meditation are better suited for different people.

I know a man who struggled for years to progress in strictly contentless meditation. He was never successful. But he becomes absolutely ecstatic when dancing or doing physical exercise. He finally realized that such physical activities are his appropriate path to spiritual integration, and he has wisely given up trying to force himself to meditate. He is the kind of person who would achieve deep spiritual experience davening (performing rocking prayer) at the Jewish synagogue, or spinning dizzily with Muslim dervishes, or processing with Christians around shrines, or making Hindu pilgrimages to holy places.

However, most people, and especially those at the early stages of spiritual integration, benefit from techniques that access the spirit through the psyche: discursive, affective, and imageful meditation. So much is this the case that, for most people, satisfying religion and spiritual fulfillment involve things like inspiring words, insightful thoughts, moving experiences, and imaginative fancies. People flock to hear inspiring preachers. People long for religion that moves them emotionally. They even talk of "experiencing God" and being "consoled by God" when they feel good in a spiritual context. And when the feelings run out and religious practice gets dull, they speak of spiritual "dryness" and a "dark night of the soul."

I find that religion brings God into such things all too easily. Why should only positive emotions be associated with God? Why should one believe God is no longer present just because one is no longer feeling inspired? Why should one's spiritual pursuits revolve around an effort to induce uplifting feelings? These questions should make it obvious that identifying inner experiences with the experience of God is problematic at best. When emotion and inspiration and new insight cease, has God ceased to be present? The answer is obviously no. Yet most religion is invested in making people feel good; most preaching labors to come up with an original idea; and most people identify spiritual experience with such things.

As people mature, work through their "hang-ups" and become psychologically healthy and religiously sophisticated, it becomes harder and harder for them to find inspiration in religion. They've seen it all before; they've already heard it—been there, done that. Exciting novelty is hard to come by in the spiritual realm.

My own move from preached retreats to silent, Buddhist

meditative retreats came from just such a growth process. After a certain point, like Eliza Doolittle in *My Fair Lady,* I was saying to myself, "Words, words, words! I'm so sick of words." I had studied enough theology and psychology that I was unlikely to find a preacher genuinely interesting on an intellectual level. I had undergone enough psychological counseling that my emotional life was basically even-keeled. So most standard religion came across to me as dull and flat. It was no longer meeting my spiritual needs; it was no longer contributing to my personal growth.

When standard religion and formal piety no longer work, you have reached an important milestone in your spiritual life. The spiritual masters in the Western tradition all speak of this turning point. The Eastern masters presume this turning point as their starting point; they understand it as the beginning of a true spiritual quest. And all the masters recommend that at this point a person should begin contentless meditation, moving beyond thoughts, feelings, and images and entering into purely spiritual experience. Thus, for many people, perhaps most, who are serious about spirituality, contentless meditative practice must eventually become a regular part of their lives. If you are at this stage in your own life, my advice is to remember that different kinds of meditation fit different people, and the same people may need different meditations at different times in their spiritual quest. It is important to know which kind of meditation to practice and when to switch tracks.

We Are All Three Elements

Given that there are three accesses to the human spirit, there is a second implication to consider. Different accesses are appropriate to different people and to the same person at different times. Yet the unity of the tripartite human being implies that meditative experience itself is unlikely ever to be purely of only one kind. Since the person is body, psyche, and spirit, somehow these three will all be involved in whatever a person does. Obviously, for example, even the most subtle, purely spiritual effects of a meditative practice occur in a human being—who exists in a body and bears an emotionally charged history. The spirit is ever connected with the body and the psyche.

Of course, some will insist that they literally "leave the body" and have purely spiritual experiences apart from the functioning of the organic brain and the sustaining structures of the human psyche. I am unsympathetic to such statements taken literally, and for serious reasons: such statements suppose that human beings are really just spirits somehow encased or imprisoned in bodies, that the supreme goal of life is to free oneself from the body and the physical world, and, in the extreme, that the physical world is merely an illusion and the "really real" exists in some "spiritual" realm beyond ordinary experience or knowledge.

Not only do such suppositions fly in the face of the evidence; they also entail blatant self-contradiction. Making knowledge claims about the absolute reality of some supposed other-worldly realm, these suppositions impugn the reality of this world—even though these impugning claims are made in this world. Thus, the argument simultaneously presumes and rejects the ultimate reality of this world; the argument simultaneously affirms and denies the validity of this world. To take these claims seriously, one must grant the validity of claims made in this world, yet the claims themselves deny the ultimacy of anything in this world. The claims are self-discrediting.

Such other-worldly, body-denying spirituality is technically called dualism. It is the hallmark of most Eastern thought; in the West it characterizes some forms of Platonism as well as

Gnosticism; and through Neoplatonism during the formative Christian centuries, it came to characterize Christianity. As a result, most Americans, when pressed, admit that they believe we are really minds or souls encased in bodies, come from some other-worldly realm, temporarily passing through this world, and are destined to return to "heaven," leaving their bodies in the earth. This belief is so commonplace that it is taken for granted even by Christians who claim still to believe in the resurrection of the body, or by Jews whose profoundly honest tradition can hardly conceive of life after death—simply because, in both cases, life without a body could hardly be a human life at all.

The self-contradiction of dualism was part of the confusion I experienced in my spiritual quest as a seminarian. Now I can understand what was going on. Insistence on a spiritual realm appealed to vague things like "grace" and the "supernatural" to account for spiritual experiences—as if these experiences were extraordinary and not fully natural human phenomena. The implication was that spiritual advancement required getting to some other place—instead of learning to be present in the here and now. Religious commitment to these beliefs allowed the confusion to go unchallenged. Talk of being "in the world but not of the world" tries to finesse the matter. But actually I was confused and many others also were and still are.

The human being is a unity, one total reality. Within the human we can analytically distinguish body, psyche, and spirit; but it must be impossible to physically separate these three and still have a human being. The spirit alone is not the person; neither is the body nor the psyche. Then, what happens at death? According to the Christianized Neoplatonic notion, death is the "separation of body and soul" and the "return of the soul to heaven." But if at death only one facet of the person, the spirit or the soul, "goes to heaven" and the body goes into the grave, where does the person go? Remember that the person is the body and the psyche as well as the spirit. This question is not easy to answer. Most patently, it leaves death a mystery and requires us to live in death's shadow, something that all of us are reluctant to do: hence, the popularity of simplistic religion. Living honestly with the unknowns of human life is a major challenge for authentic spirituality. I will address this matter in more detail in part 3. Here my point is that the human being is a unity, a complex composite of body, psyche, and spirit—not any one of these elements alone.

Some Practices Engage the Three Elements

The fact that the human being is body, psyche, and spirit has a third implication, one immediately relevant to the practice of meditation. Religious practice or ritual that builds in all three accesses to the spirit can be especially effective. Any good religious service will include occasions to engage the body, the psyche, and the spirit: there will be physical involvement such as required postures, movements, and gestures; there will be imaginative and emotional triggers such as good preaching, music, or pageantry; and there will be long moments of complete silence, time for undistracted experience of the spirit.

The Catholic rosary provides an interesting example. Through the fingering of strung beads and the verbal enunciation of the prayers, the rosary engages the body. The "mysteries" (incidents in the life of Jesus and Mary) assigned to the sets of prescribed prayers provide topics for discursive, affective, and imageful meditation—matters of the psyche. And the hypnotic repetition of the *Ave* functions as a mantra, one technique of contentless meditation, to quiet the mind and open the soul to moments of pure spiritual presence. People make a gross mistake—like the magical misunderstanding of spirituality that I encountered in my seminary days—in thinking that, while praying the rosary, one is to be attentive over and over again to the words of the repeated *Ave*. The point of the rosary is not to pray the Hail Mary fifty or one hundred and fifty times in a row, but to use the repetition to induce an altered state of consciousness, to access the human spirit in a variety of ways, and, thus, to facilitate deeper modes of prayer.

When it comes to using techniques for meditation, however, it is important to try and keep them distinct. It is important not to haphazardly mix the techniques for access through the body and psyche with the techniques for direct access to the spirit. The next chapter introduces a technique that effects this direct access.

CHAPTER 5

A Technique for Meditation

⌒⌒

WHEN I WAS IN SEMINARY, I used to get stir-crazy during long, silent retreats. Thoughts in my head would go round and round. I experienced no insight, no inspiration, no consolation. I was just bored and frustrated. What I lacked was a technique to tame my restless mind and to open myself up to the pure experience of my spirit. I was surrounded by silence, but I needed a method to make good use of the silence with which I was dealing. Unfortunately, nobody knew such a method, or, if somebody did, nobody was telling. All I heard was talk of "grace" and "spiritual favors" that "God" might "grant" to those who were "worthy" or "specially chosen."

I waited in vain.

As it turns out, silence plays a key role in all spiritual pursuit, and especially in the practice of meditation. In silence one can move beyond thoughts, emotions, and images and come to rest at peace in an experience of mere presence, just being there. Religious traditions have developed techniques to facilitate this process.

Here I introduce one such technique—just one. I offer it as part of a "starter's kit" for those seriously committed to the spiritual quest. Of course, there are many such techniques available, and you can waste your time trying them all. You can skip from this one to that in pursuit of some magical formula that will save you from life's hardships and bring you to some fancied state of spiritual bliss. But the search for that single, perfect technique is a trap. That search just delays getting down to serious work. One technique is all that is needed. The perfect technique is the one that you use religiously, and the one that you use religiously is the one that works.

> I have no faith in the magical power of mere words.
> What is important is the inner repetition
> of a constant word or sound.

The technique I offer involves the internal repetition of a word. In a Christian form this technique is the method of Centering Prayer, developed by the Trappist monks at Spencer Abbey in Massachusetts and based on the medieval spiritual classic *The Cloud of Unknowing*. This same technique, as far as I know, occurs in the Transcendental Meditation (TM) popularized in the United States by Maharishi Mahesh Yogi. Variations on this technique are commonplace in the religious traditions, as I will illustrate later.

Choice of a Word

First, this spiritual practice requires choosing some word or perhaps a couple of short words—simpler is better—to use as a mantra. *Mantra* is the technical Eastern term for such a word or series of words that, like a magic formula, is proclaimed in order to achieve some desired result. The term *mantra* is also used to refer to a brief formula that is repeated as part of a spiritual practice like the one I am describing. The use of mantras is a distinguishing feature of a form of Tibetan Buddhism sometimes called *mantrayana*. For the meditative practice that I am suggesting, a word that has personal meaning is useful—like love, peace, trust, rest, let go, relax, let God, release, be here.

In accord with mantrayana belief, some teachers insist that the word itself is important. The claim is that particular words have spiritual power and that the specific sound of the word matters. Supposedly, some sounds are more effective than others, and some sounds effect one result, and others, another.

This peculiar belief in the power of declaimed formulas is evident among biblical fundamentalists. They believe that simply proclaiming a biblical passage releases a spiritual power that can change or convert people. There is a similar emphasis on the power of words in the Jewish cabalistic tradition. One focuses on words, repeats them, mulls them over, relates them to one another, and finds in the very verbal structure of the scriptures a supposed source of revelation and healing. In fact, in many religious traditions words used in specific situations are believed to have power.

I have no faith in the magical power of mere words. Likewise, I do not believe that the use of this or that word in itself is ultimately important for effective meditation, although some sounds may set up resonance in the brain more easily than others. In fact, thinking about the meaning of your word during the meditative practice constitutes distraction from the exercise of the meditation, so the meaning of the word should not matter and should not come into play during meditation. What is important is the inner repetition of a constant word or sound. Nonetheless, use of a personally meaningful word might provide added motivation to continue your practice. So you must choose some mantra.

Repetition of the Word

Second, begin repeating the word in your mind and eventually get to the point where "the word repeats itself." That is, this process is to go on rather automatically, effortlessly. It is important that meditation not be a matter of pushing and forcing, but one of gentleness, ease, and letting go. Rigorously determined effort to keep the word in repetition, come what may, is counterproductive. The goal during meditation is not to go on forcing experience to be what we want, but, at least during the minutes of meditation, to relax, stand back, and let things be what they will.

Return to the Word

Third, your mind will inevitably drift from the word, and eventually you will catch yourself drifting. Whenever you become aware that you have drifted from the word, acknowledge the drifting and gently return to the word.

I speak of "drifting," not "distraction." Although I did loosely use the word *distraction* above, here I speak more accurately. The drifting is not a distraction. In religious circles the word *distraction* often carries negative and guilt-laden connotations: "Don't be distracted during your prayer!" But the drifting of the mind is a natural and inevitable part of meditative practice. In fact, the drifting is an essential part. Without the drifting, you would not have the opportunity to practice coming back to your word. This coming back is central to meditation. Each time you need to come back to your word, you not only learn about your mind's wanderings and notice which things catch its attention; you also have a chance to strengthen your habit of being present, a chance to become more deliberately aware of what you are doing. Thus, use of the mantra serves to facilitate increased awareness.

While avoiding pure self-indulgence, be gentle with yourself in this process. Do not be critical of yourself because your mind drifts. And gently take note of what your mind drifts toward. After all, these matters would not be arising in your mind if somehow they were not important to you. Be kind to your driftings. They matter to you. At the same time, during your meditation practice gently let go of the driftings: meditation time is not the time for those things.

Variations on the Technique

The meditation technique that I proposed depends on a common mechanism, the use of some anchor to bring awareness back from its driftings. Other techniques employ this same mechanism but use things other than a mantra as the anchor. One alternative approach, simple yet powerful, is to sit silently while maintaining awareness of the beating of your heart. Another practice is to follow the inhalation and exhalation of your breathing. An aurally oriented technique would fix attention on some constant sound. The practice of sitting silently near a creek, a brook, or the ocean and attending to the rush of the water is an example of this aural technique. A visually oriented technique would focus sight on some object—a candle flame, a sacred icon or statue, a rosebud, a spot on the wall. The mandala in the East and the rose window in the West provide objects specifically made for use in visually oriented meditation.

As I realized only later, I had been using that visual technique all my Catholic life. The devotion of Adoration of the Blessed Sacrament—unfortunately never understood and so, now virtually unused—involved that technique. The Eucharistic host, about three inches in diameter, was set upon the altar for veneration, held up to view in an ornate and jeweled monstrance or ostensorium. The monstrance, including a stand, was usually circular in shape and often had the four arms of the cross and additional golden "rays" radiating out from the host at the center. In accord with Catholic emphasis on the consecrated host, the monstrance was designed to highlight it. At the same time, however, this design drew the viewer's gaze ever back to the center as, for long minutes and sometimes for hours at a time, the believer knelt before the Eucharist in silent prayer. This Catholic devotion had all the essential elements of meditative practice—silence, posture, ritual, and, of course, an anchor of focused awareness. Practicing this devotion as millions of other innocents had done before me, I was doing meditation for years before I even knew the term.

I note these variations on the core meditative mechanism only to further understanding of how meditation works. Again I repeat my warning of not to be switching from one technique to another in an effort to seem spiritually knowledgeable or to keep meditative practice interesting. In general, one needs to choose one technique and stick with it.

There are other practical considerations to be mentioned about meditative practice. The following chapter presents them.

CHAPTER 6

Some Practical Considerations about Meditation

OUR MINDS SEEM OFTEN to be their own boss. They jump and flit from this thing to that, and we have little control over them. They leave us in a whirl, unable to focus. Over the centuries the religious traditions have developed techniques for taming the restless mind. In chapter 5 I described one such technique. That technique includes three steps: choosing a word, repeating the word mentally, and returning your attention to the word whenever you catch your mind drifting. In this chapter I relate some other things to remember if you are planning to use that meditative technique.

Timing and Posture

In general, do this practice about twenty minutes at a stretch. Twice per day would be ideal. You could use this technique for longer periods, perhaps a half hour or so, but extended practice is not recommended. The process of meditation is a long-term one. As I will explain in part 2, the process actually works by gradually dismantling and restructuring the mind. You do not want to push the process. From this point of view, meditation is like bodybuilding. If you work out every day, you need to alternate the muscle groups that you exercise. The muscles need a day to rest and rebuild. Similarly, hasty dismantling of the mind, without leaving time for its healthy restructuring, might leave it lying in pieces. Meditative techniques, simple as they sound, are psychologically powerful. They are not to be toyed with.

Proper posture is also an important part of meditative practice. All the religious traditions have required ritual postures, and the common element is maintenance of an erect spine. Egyptian ritual has one sit erect in a chair with hands placed on the knees. Jewish ritual posture is standing erect. Christians kneel upright or kneel back resting on a seat or on their heels. Eastern posture is the cross-legged, seated, lotus position that has both feet wrapped up and resting on the opposite leg. Native American posture is another kind of crossed-legged sitting that leaves the feet under the legs. In every case, the erect spine keeps you focused and allows for unobstructed breathing.

It is important to find a comfortable meditation position and to stick with it. Sometimes the most you can do during your meditation time is to keep yourself in position. This exercise is itself a valuable discipline.

During meditation you should be in a relaxed but alert position. Going to extreme in either direction is not helpful. Too much rigidity sets up restrictive tensions. Too much relaxation induces sleep. Don't kid yourself that you are meditating while lying down; you are resting or napping—although I have heard of people with painful back conditions who do successfully meditate while lying flat on the floor.

I chuckle—and sometimes shudder—to recall the story of a religious woman who thanked God that she was not hurt in an auto accident. She explained that she escaped injury probably because she was very relaxed when the accident occurred: she had been meditating as she drove down the road! I wondered if she would not have avoided the accident altogether had she kept her mind on her driving. And I wonder how serious a meditation she could have been doing while driving a car. Despite her religious enthusiasm, her mobile meditative maneuvers were certainly misguided.

Meditation is a specific practice that requires specific procedures. It is something to be set apart from other daily activities, something to be done on its own and for its own sake. It is important to set aside specific times for meditation and, as best you can, to meditate regularly. And do it before eating, not after eating, because the digestive process directs the blood to the stomach and intestines and conflicts with the circulation to the brain that is needed for the mental work of meditation.

Of course, you can use "down time" for meditation practice—while sitting in a waiting room, waiting for an airplane, or even riding a bus or train. Often I will meditate in my car when I arrive early for an appointment or when I just need to get away somewhere and find some space. Using these makeshift situations is not ideal. For example, I do much better sitting shoeless on the floor in half-lotus position with a cushion under my butt than trying to maintain proper posture in a car or airplane seat. Having a regular place, procedure, and time for meditation is the better approach; making your meditation practice into a ritual is ideal. Nonetheless, better to meditate when you can find a stray opportunity than not to meditate at all.

Being Present

The same single-mindedness that surrounds the externals of meditation practice also pertains to the internal practice. The goal of meditation is to be present to the moment and to use the mantra to facilitate that presence. Accordingly, during meditative practice every thought, image, and feeling is but another drifting of the mind and ought to be recognized and treated as such.

Sometimes profound thoughts and significant insights occur when you are meditating—precisely because you are relaxed and your mind is open. Still, no matter how interesting or penetrating an idea might be, it is still just another "thought," a drifting of the mind away from contentless, open awareness. This thought and every other should be gently but firmly dismissed. If your ideas are truly significant and relevant, they will recur. To pursue them with prolonged analysis is to abandon meditating, no matter how "spiritual" their content. To think about the meaning of your mantra or your life, to begin wondering why you are even doing this practice, to begin thinking of God, or even to start speaking to God in prayer—all is but a drifting of the mind. Such mental pursuits may be proper to discursive meditation, but they do not belong in contentless meditation.

Even apart from all talk of God, our inner selves are more expansive than we realize.

The same must be said about feelings or images that arise in the mind. These may be powerfully enjoyable or intriguingly interesting. But during meditation they, too, are but driftings of the mind. They belong in affective or imageful meditation, but they are not part of contentless meditation.

People who speak of meditation in a religious context, who discuss meditation as a way of relating to God, make the same point: any thought about God or feeling toward God is only one's own thought or feeling; it is not God. Thoughts and feelings *about* God are not God. In prayer the goal is to actually make contact with God. We make contact with God by being present to the here-and-now wherein God is and acts. Thinking and feeling about God or about anything else—the yesterdays and tomorrows, the if-only's and what-if's, the ruminations and planning—are a distraction from the present moment; they are always at least one step removed from experience itself. Therefore, when contentless meditation is understood as a form of prayer relating one to God, even the most sublime thoughts and most moving emotions need to be gently dismissed. From this point of view, interesting ideas and consoling emotions present a seduction; they lure us away from the pure and immediate presence to God. They tempt us to substitute our petty ideas and self-indulgent emotions for the Infinite and Incomprehensible Source of the Universe. They dupe us into believing that we actually understand the Ultimate Mystery, the Great Unknown.

I used the words *petty* and *self-indulgent,* but I do not want to make anyone feel guilty. I merely want to highlight this fact: even apart from all talk of God, our inner selves are more expansive than we realize. We are more than we generally know. Settling down into our thoughts and emotions short-circuits the movement to broader openness of our minds and hearts. Far from being petty and self-centered, our deepest being is unbounded openness to the universe. Such virtually infinite potential is what we are. Thoughts, images, and feelings, even about God, are dismissed because to hold onto them is to sell ourselves short.

In fact, pursuing thoughts, emotions, and images while in a state of deep meditation can be dangerous. Like the Sirens that tempted Odysseus, psychodynamic materials—images, memories, emotions—rising from one's inner depths can seduce a meditator. In the extreme, one can get lost in the labyrinth of the psyche, be taken up with bizarre thoughts and longed-for emotions, become obsessed with irrational schemes and senseless fears, or even suffer mental breakdown. Wanting to indulge in the Sirens' song, Odysseus had himself safely tied to the mast of his ship. Similarly, in meditation the mantra serves as a secure center post, and holding to it allows one to navigate the straits of the psyche without getting caught in the tangles of one's mind.

Techniques of contentless meditation require dismissing from the mind all thoughts, emotions, and images regardless of how appealing they might be. Nonetheless, I must confess, at times I have broken this rule. Sometimes, when during meditation I remember something that really needs attention, I will open my eyes, pick up one of my shoes, toss it across the room, and then go back to my meditation. Afterward, needing to retrieve the shoe reminds me of what I had remembered during meditation. On some few occasions over many years, I have actually taken a pad and pencil and jotted down some idea that came to me. Throwing the shoe or making a quick note allows me to let go of those thoughts and get back to my meditation while still being able to retrieve important thoughts when my meditation is over.

I do not officially recommend taking such liberties with the meditative technique. Perhaps if I were more adept at meditation, I would realize that nothing whatsoever is more important than "getting back to one's word" and eventually achieving "an enlightened mind." Perhaps I would realize that nothing justifies opening one's eyes or taking pencil to paper in the middle of meditation. But I am not at that supposed ideal state. I wonder if anyone is—or even should be.

I remember Jesus' teaching that, if on the way to worship you remember that a brother or sister has something against you, you are to leave your gift at the altar, go reconcile with that sister or brother, and only then return to offer your gift: some things are more important than one's personal pieties and a supposed quest for enlightenment. Or as Jesus said elsewhere, "The Sabbath was made for humankind, not humankind for the Sabbath" (Mark 2:27). Meditation is to serve life, not vice versa. Real-life concerns often trump piety and religious practices.

Wholesome living overall is the bottom line of all spirituality. As I said in the first paragraph of this book, I no longer worry about becoming a saint: these days I just try to be a good person.

Beginning and Ending

Moving from the hurly-burly of everyday life into the stillness of meditation sometimes takes a few minutes. It is helpful to begin meditation with some brief relaxation exercise. Before beginning repetition of your mantra, set yourself solidly in your meditation position and take about five deep breaths. Hold each breath for five or ten seconds, and slowly exhale. This simple breathing exercise serves nicely to calm oneself. No wonder the yogic tradition puts so much emphasis on body posture and controlled breathing. The Lamaze method of childbirth builds on the same wisdom.

Also expect that it may sometimes take five or ten minutes of working with your mantra before the "automatic pilot" of meditative process kicks in. It takes a while to get into the meditative space. And on some occasions, you will just never get there. But life goes on anyway, and the moments you spend attempting to meditate—practicing—are, indeed, what the practice of meditation is about. Believe it or not, just by sitting there for your allotted time, you have made progress.

I deliberately choose to wear a cheap Casio watch equipped

with an alarm. In this way, no matter where I am, I can set the alarm for 20 minutes and do my meditation without preoccupation about the time. Certainly, opening one's eyes periodically to glance at a clock is not conducive to meditation. Some people develop a rather precise sense of when their meditation time is up, so they do without a timer. I find that the experience of meditation varies so starkly from one time to another that I cannot depend on my internal sense of time, nor do I see any particular virtue in being able to do so.

It is useful to take a few minutes for coming out of the meditative state. This would be the time for thinking about life's issues, for reciting a favorite prayer or inspirational piece, for reading some thought for the day, or for just sitting in silence for a few moments more. Sometimes I sing a favorite hymn or a piece of Gregorian chant—*Veni Creator Spiritus, Jesu Dulcis Memoria, Te Deum*—and in this way to some extent I reconnect my current spirituality with my Christian tradition and Catholic upbringing. I also find that the music elicits an emotional response that enriches the experience of pure meditation. After one's contentless meditation is finished, then is the time for discursive, affective, or imageful meditation. In these matters, one's actions should be deliberate.

Other Advice

The immediate effects of meditation vary from person to person and for the same person from day to day. It is not helpful to project what those effects "should" be, for then we go on to try and achieve such effects. We force the matter, and in the process we distort the very essence of the spiritual quest: if anything, it requires open-mindedness and receptivity to whatever might be, not some hard-nosed determination to make something in particular happen.

In part 2 I will detail what the overall, long-term effects of meditation are likely to be. But such statements must be generic, and they should be taken with a grain of salt. The mystics' descriptions of spiritual experiences sound fascinating and appealing: enlightenment, mystical experience, union with the all, ecstasy, bliss, total openness. Yet the uninitiated will inevitably mistake what these descriptions mean in the living. The uninitiated will also tend to overlook the other, ominous, and parallel descriptions that run through all the spiritual traditions: experience of the void, dark night of the soul, surgery without an anesthetic, emptiness, nothingness.

Mystical experience is not all that it is popularly cracked up to be. Much of what is proposed as spiritual—the visions, voices, raptures, intuitions—is actually the result of psychological and neurological pathology. I learned this fact only when I began doing psychological research on spiritual experiences, only after many naïve years of belief that one should admire, prize, and seek extraordinary experiences. And much else of the supposed spiritual is but inventive fiction or outright deception that distracts us from the challenge of living and inflates the pocketbooks and egos of media-savvy gurus.

One very common—and hardly exotic—effect of meditation is that you fall asleep! So maintain your posture as best you can, and remain vigilant: keep your mind on the inner task at hand; practice being mindful. If you find that you fall asleep regularly during meditation, you are probably sleep-deprived and should adjust your daily schedule to give yourself more sleep.

Other common effects of meditation can also be mentioned. Sometimes it is good to know what to expect so you do not worry about being "normal"—though anybody committed to the practice of meditation should get over any preoccupation with being normal. We are all different, and we change from moment to moment.

During meditation some people experience profound relaxation while others get increasingly anxious or fearful or sad or giddy, and still others experience a "rush" or sense of floating while others note nothing at all. Of course, during meditation any and all of these experiences should simply be acknowledged and gently dismissed. In no case should one be striving to hold on to an experience. One should rather let the experience arise and pass as it will. In fact, the very letting go of affirming experiences actually enhances the meditation—because the overall process is precisely an exercise in letting go. So in meditation one need never fear losing something positive by releasing it. This same lesson might also apply to many things in life—a person whom one loves, for example.

The popular notion that spiritually advanced
people live blissful lives is mistaken.

In fact, the real results of meditation do not manifest themselves during the meditative exercise. They show later in the day. You may note you have more energy or, on another occasion, you'll feel lethargic. Other days you will find yourself inexplicably impatient and irritable, or maybe happy and playful. These changes in emotion and mood result from shifts in the psyche facilitated by meditation. Especially in the early stages of meditative practice, until some degree of inner stability is achieved, such affective shifts are an inevitable part of meditative practice. And why not? They are also an inevitable part of ordinary daily living. Is meditation supposed to somehow preserve us from life's ups and downs? On the contrary, meditation intensifies the experience of living.

As we will see later, meditation does its work by loosening the structures of the psyche, so that whatever is buried there may emerge because of meditation. The result is not always pleasant. Said otherwise, meditative practice moves us deeply into the experience of life, and life is a mixed bag. As I noted earlier, the popular notion that spiritually advanced people live blissful lives is mistaken. If anything, they merely learn to keep an even keel while deeply experiencing and successfully negotiating the ups and downs of life. Paradoxically, they learn to delight in life, which, by its very nature, includes hardships. So the delight is there, but the challenges do not magically go away.

Meditative practice and spiritual growth are not just about how we spend twenty minutes twice a day. They are about life and how we live it. The next two chapters pursue this further topic.

CHAPTER 7

Silence in Social Settings

ONE DAY IN HIGH SCHOOL, I was helping Sister Eugene carry some things to the convent. With youthful idealism and naïve understanding, I revealed to her that I was thinking of becoming a Trappist. The Trappists—the Order of Cistercians of the Strict Observance, famous for Thomas Merton—maintain strict and perpetual silence as well as other austerities. Sister Eugene stopped in her tracks, turned, and upbraided me.

"Daniel," she said.

Nobody called me Daniel at that time; I was either Danny or, increasingly, Dan.

"Daniel," she said. "How dare you speak that way! You're going to lock yourself away in a monastery? With all your talents, you should be serving the Lord in more productive ways."

I am ever grateful for her stark lesson in spiritual realism.

In the last decades of the twentieth century, others were also professing a more down-to-earth spirituality—but, I am sure, not always with the genuineness of Sister Eugene. With new religious justifications, people questioned virginity and celibacy, social activism became a religious ideal, and silence was no longer part of spiritual retreats. Fortunately, my experience with the Buddhists and my study of psychology provided me with a new appreciation of silence.

Not only spiritually inclined people but also thoughtful people in general have recognized the value of silence: "Speech is silver; silence is golden." "Silence is as deep as eternity" (Thomas Carlyle). "They approach nearest to the gods who know how to be silent" (Cato the Elder). Even outside of meditation times, silence is a useful tool for fostering spiritual integration.

The traditional religious retreat was conducted in silence for days and weeks at a time, and, as a seminarian and priest, I made many such retreats. But in my experience, there was little understanding of why silence was to be maintained. Anemic religious reasons were given: one was to avoid worldly distractions, and one was to be open to God—as if God is not present in the everyday world.

The Imitation of Christ, a late-medieval spiritual classic, insisted repeatedly that most conversation is worthless: social intercourse leaves us the worse, so it is better to avoid other people. This pessimistic, other-worldly spirituality reigned into the mid-twentieth century. Activities "in this world" were considered inferior to "the things of God." We were to "live for heaven" and "flee the world." Marriage, business, politics, conversation, friendship—all were considered less worthy than the explicit pursuit of the spiritual. For this reason, some religious communities once lived in perpetual silence, and for this reason the retreats I attended in years past were conducted in silence.

Silence Lost and Gained

In fact, the physical world itself used to be a quieter place. In a world filled with cars, trucks, trains, planes, emergency sirens, and construction projects, we—especially those of us who live in the city—seldom hear real silence. When I visited the Grand

Canyon, I was awed by its silence and sat entranced on the rim. Perhaps more than the canyon itself, the silence opened onto a world of seemingly infinite expanse. Thus, for me, the Grand Canyon was a distinctly spiritual experience.

In the last generation, we have filled what little silence was left in our world with chatter—TV, radio, cell phones, computers— proving the antisocial medievals correct. We now seldom experience true silence. Keeping the conversation going, filling the "dead air time," has become a contemporary social responsibility. People seem unable to walk down a street, survey the aisles of a grocery store, or drive an expressway without talking to someone on cell phones. Are we afraid to be alone with ourselves?

Theology is irrelevant to the matter of silence, and talk of the wickedness of the world is a dangerous oversimplification.

Yet only in moments of patient silence and with slow-paced conversation are we really able to plumb our souls and begin to reveal our hearts. Every good psychotherapist knows the importance of giving the client space to experience and finally express him- or herself. The things of the heart are subtle, sometimes difficult to call forth, and always hard to put into words. As in a city under siege, bombardment of the mind by external stimuli prevents internal movement, minimizes psychic shifting, and forbids the emergence of psychodynamically relevant material. When all efforts are directed toward external response, no attention can be given to internal experience. Despite widespread psychological awareness in our day, apart from the rare heart-to-heart conversation, we give one another little silent time to explore our souls in conversation, and we allow ourselves little silent time to know our own hearts.

Silence that is rich—solitude, not loneliness—fosters the

unearthing of the psyche. Regular meditation is one means of keeping other moments of silence rich. Then inner change can occur; restructuring of the psyche can ensue. Then more coherent integration of the spirit into the structures of the psyche can result. This is the way in which spiritual growth proceeds, so this psychological analysis explains the potential value in silence. Apart from suggesting to believers that God is somehow behind the process—because God is somehow behind everything—theology is irrelevant to the matter of silence, and talk of the wickedness of the world is a dangerous oversimplification.

Stepping out of Social Roles

Solitude triggers another mechanism that is conducive to spiritual integration: the short-circuiting of superficial, social reinforcement. The song "A Horse with No Name" by America contains this line: "In the desert you can't remember your name, for there ain't no one for to give you no pain." I take this line to mean that social interaction often keeps us from knowing who we really are. We play games with one another, and the games are unconscious. We categorize one another and through our stereotypical responses keep one another in the identity boxes we have created.

Every family, for example, projects certain roles onto its members. The one is the family clown, the other, the serious one; this one is invisible, and that one is the socialite. For whatever reasons—sometimes for sheer survival's sake and certainly because of native talent and spontaneous interests—we adopt certain social strategies. We begin living in what Carl Jung called our "persona," the mask with which we present ourselves to the outside world, the "personality" we wear like a garment in a public setting. And social interaction within the public setting works to keep everyone in his and her place. The social system imposes its roles and keeps people in them.

Watch how any new group forms—a budding circle of friends, people at a weekend workshop, a dozen loose acquaintances celebrating a birthday around a dinner table. The patterns emerge and solidify quickly. Each one takes or is forced into particular roles. When the conversation lulls, for example, everyone looks to the jokester or the leader to open a new line of talk while the shy or quiet ones are allowed to sit back in their passive observation.

We do not generally experience this social pressure as an imposition. We actually welcome it. It lets us know where we stand and how we are to behave. It sustains our identity. It helps us define who we are. It spares us the effort of becoming our own unique selves. Of course, at times we do feel boxed in, and then we rebel: we struggle to assert a new role and a new social identity.

Mechanisms of social identity can be at work in the most casual encounters. A passing nod or simple "Good morning" makes us feel we fit in. For example, waking up with, or at the call of, another person is very different from waking up alone. The presence of other people quickly draws us into the world of social consensus. Our dreams, our early morning restlessness, our anxious fretting over the day's challenges, all the mysterious, disturbing, and fascinating chaos of our deep, inner selves—we forget all this and engage in proper social interaction.

Even apart from waking moments, contact with another person draws us out of our inner world. A stranger's simple "Hello" that catches us day-dreaming brings us back to "reality." Add a title to the greeting—"Good morning, Mrs. So-and-so," "Hello, Dr. Such-and-such"—and it becomes more obvious how simply acknowledging another person can innocently but nonetheless powerfully enforce social identities and stereotypes.

Some time ago I had a leak in my condo bathroom. Water was dripping from the ceiling. I contacted the maintenance staff to investigate the problem. It turned out that the water was coming from two floors above mine. I had gone with the maintenance man, Shirah, to check things out and to be of what help I could. I helped with the water vacuum equipment and listened for water drips as he attempted various maneuvers. I was caught up short as we parted and he said, "Well, Professor, I guess that's about all we can do for today."

Professor? I am not used to hearing that title. Besides, I hadn't thought of myself as a professor while I was helping find the leak. I thought of myself as the do-it-yourself kind of guy that I grew up as alongside my dad, brother, and uncles, all quite adept at making repairs around the house. In my mind, I was just being "one of the guys." So at Shirah's comment, I felt like an outsider, someone of special status, a person in a different category. I guess that, from Shirah's point of view, I am in a different category: I am an owner, and he is the maintenance man. But I did not want to be in that category in that particular instance. His polite and proper address actually boxed me into an identity that I was not feeling at that time. Had he called me Daniel—that is, just little ol' me, for whatever I am—I would have felt much more affirmed.

The greetings we use are often addressed to the person whom everyone knows us to be. Greetings are often made to social roles, to personas. Thus, even innocent greetings define and enforce social stereotypes.

What happens when people do not acknowledge one another nor exchange expected greetings? What happens when people impose silence on the social scene? This is exactly what happens on a silent retreat. Then we are free to shed our roles. We no longer need to summon up the energy required to maintain the mask we are expected to wear. Then we are free to begin thinking of ourselves in novel ways and to begin feeling the spontaneous inklings that rise up within ourselves. Then we are required to start being with ourselves. And upsurgings of unfamiliar energies released from our depths are likely to make surprising things happen when we return to the social arena.

The suspension of conventional patterns of social interaction allows for new personal exploration and personal restructuring. This restructuring, in turn, allows for the integration of one's built-in spiritual urges. Thus, silence can be an effective device for fostering spiritual growth.

My experience in other countries and cultures was enlightening on this score. I believe American society is particularly compulsive about our need to acknowledge and greet one another. Sometimes the practice becomes annoying and even laughable as we say hello over and over again when, throughout the day, we repeatedly pass, say, work colleagues or neighbors. Yet, if we omit the greeting, we or the other feel uncomfortable and begin to wonder, "What's wrong?"

Other peoples are not so neurotic, not so dependent on constant social reinforcement. When I lived at the Scots College in Rome, my first year was particularly difficult. Not only was I far from home—I was extracted from my own culture. I felt isolated and ignored. I did not feel affirmed. After some time, when I was communicating more openly with my Scottish mates, I spoke of my feelings of isolation during that first year. I was surprised at their response. Far from ignoring or disliking me, I was told, they had quickly sized me up and respected me highly. As a result, they didn't want to intrude on me, so they left me to myself, they "gave me my space." This was the Scottish way of acknowledging someone: allowing him to be himself. Evidently, I was still too insecure, still too American, to be able to appreciate the tribute.

There can be a gesture of respect in not addressing a person.

When we feel awe or admiration for some great personage, we often stand back, feeling unworthy to make direct, personal contact. Not addressing another person, but maintaining silence, can be a way of showing deference to the mystery of the other, to the unique and unpredictable individuality of each person. The widespread Asian custom of bowing to another person with folded hands seems to embody this sense of reverence toward a person. Although Asian societies are also hemmed round with layers of protocol, the reverence in their greeting ritual can be taken to express an openness that leaves the other free to become him- or herself, for whatever that might mean.

Again, the lesson of silence comes through: words and obligatory social rituals—even as they support and reassure us—confine and restrict our persons. Social interaction is a trade-off. Periods of silence can unleash our spirits and open us to far transcendent realms. Social silence can be a tool of spiritual growth.

Other aspects of daily living—like drugs, sex, and money—also bear on the spiritual quest. The following chapter considers these.

CHAPTER 8

Other Matters of Lifestyle

R EMEMBER THE WIZARD in *The Wizard of Oz* or Obi-Wan Kenobi in *Star Wars* or Professor Dumbledore in *Harry Potter*? Just by the way they acted and dressed, you could tell they were somehow special. Whenever you see "spiritual" people in cartoons, ads, TV shows, or the movies, these people too appear in stylized form. They wear long, loose, dark robes, often with hoods, or else bright, gossamer dresses. They live in isolated forests, in hard-to-find castles, or in high mountain caves. They eat little, live austerely, and never have a companion. According to the stereotypes, the spiritual quest requires people to behave in nonstandard ways.

There is usually some bit of truth in stereotypes. In fact, ritual silence in social settings and other facets of daily living affect our spiritual growth. For this reason, spiritual traditions all have rules about lifestyle. These rules are the root of the stereotypes, but are also pointers toward wisdom.

Drugs and Alcohol

Universally, spiritual traditions forbid or strictly curtail the use of drugs, except in a ritual setting. The reason is obvious.

Drugs distort the functioning of the mind. A psychological understanding of spirituality also reveals the deeper reason. Insofar as spiritual integration is simply a matter of healthy mental life, a matter of the integration of psyche and spirit, drugs interfere with spiritual sensitivity.

Consumption of alcohol has no place on a spiritual retreat, nor should alcohol be a dominant part of a person's daily life. Alcohol fogs the mind immediately and with the hangover leaves the mind groggy for hours afterwards. The same must be said for other drugs now so commonly used in our society—marijuana, cocaine, ecstasy, crystal meth, and heroine. Caffeine and nicotine are also drugs and fall under the same indictment.

One must wonder about the health of a society in which the majority of its members need drugs—whether by prescription, over the counter, or on the street—to get through the week or the weekend. We seek out drugs because life seems intolerable without them. Indeed, our long work hours, short vacation periods, intense competition, and overall lack of inspiration and shared vision leave us in a dismal state. Americans work more than people ever have and more than people in any other nation on the face of the earth. The American way of life is a killer.

We ache for some sense of broad purpose, meaning, significance. Drugs take away the ache and provide an experience of transcendence: they make us relax, they induce a sense of well-being, they space us out, they induce altered states of consciousness. For this reason, religious rituals often employ drugs: peyote among Native Americans, ayahuasca among Brazilian tribes, wine during Jewish celebrations and Christian services. But such ritual use is a far cry from personal indulgence and addiction. Nevertheless, even on the streets and in plush back rooms the use of drugs is an attempt, a distorted and ultimately destructive attempt, to meet spiritual needs. Dedication to the spiritual path can serve the same needs in a more wholesome, productive way.

The prohibition of drug use sounds like a negative thing. It appears to come from the outside and be imposed on a person. It feels like an infringement on our freedom, on our sense of autonomy. But a deeper understanding of the matter shows that the reality is just the reverse. People who live with profound spiritual awareness spontaneously avoid drugs. Drugs of any kind cloud the mind, and spiritually alert people do not like feeling drugged. They feel happier and more alive when their minds are clear, their focus sharp. Then they are sensitive to a world of wonder and marvel all around them. They avoid or minimize their use of drugs because they enjoy life.

Comfort with one's sexuality is
important for spiritual growth. . . . It is not sex,
but sex-negativism that is the enemy
of the spirit.

Like so much else in religion, we get our message about drug use backwards. Spiritual adepts shared their wisdom about what makes life wonderful. Part of their wisdom is a negative judgment on drug use. We hear the negative judgment without having ever experienced the spiritual alertness, and we take the wisdom—morality, ethics—to be restrictive rules laid on us by uptight people. In fact, any valid "rules for living" come from the experience of living itself. And anyone actually living life intensely will come to those "rules" spontaneously. Responsibility is not something required of a person by outside authority. Responsibility names the spontaneous way of living of a person truly in love with life (chapter nineteen deals with ethics in more detail).

Sex

Besides drugs, religions tend also to be down on sex. At least Christianity is. Repeated studies of Western religion show that the more religious a person is, the more sex-negative she or he is. A further consideration is that the United States is schizophrenic over sex: the advertising industry spends millions of dollars on sexually explicit ads while a conservative presidential administration spends millions on demonstrably ineffective, "abstinence only" sex education.

More than drugs, sex is a complex thing. It requires extended discussion, and I will address it in more detail in chapter 14. Undeniable, however, is the fact that, like drugs, sex can also be used as an escape from life. It is no wonder that people often indulge in sex and drugs together.

When sex becomes a preoccupation, a diversion, a game, a perpetual chase, it does not serve personal integration, but rather the fragmentation of the self. To this extent, sex should be avoided, and especially so during periods of intense spiritual practice. Regarding the latter, Saint Paul—who actually was no prude, as becomes clear when his letters are understood within their own historical context—phrased the matter this way: "Do not deprive one another except perhaps by agreement for a set time, to devote yourselves to prayer" (1 Corinthians 7:5).

Like every good thing, sex can be abused and become spiritually destructive. Apart from all religious concern or any question of relationship with God, a psychological understanding of spiritual integration explains this fact.

By the same token, comfort with one's sexuality is important for spiritual growth. During meditative practice sexual feelings and images often arise. Sometimes as a regular turning point along the way to a deep meditative state, gentle sexual arousal occurs. I once spoke with an elderly nun who knew this phenomenon well. Fully in accord with the principles of meditative practice and fully comfortable with herself, she said that, when sexual arousal occurs during her prayer time, she thanks God for his good blessings! And then she gently lets go of the feelings and moves on with her meditation. A person uptight about sex would be thrown for a loop by sexual arousal during a spiritual practice and would probably stop meditating, fearful of sex, fleeing "temptation," running from "the devil." In fact, it is not sex, but sex-negativism that is the enemy of the spirit.

Another facet of sexuality is sexual orientation. Because I originally prepared the material in this book for presentation to a weekend retreat for gay men and because sexual orientation is, in fact, a matter of concern to everyone, I want to address this other question: What do these matters have to do with people who are gay, lesbian, bisexual, transgender, or intersex?

The simple answer is that, regardless of sexual orientation or gender identity, these matters apply to everyone equally. When the human core of spirituality is understood, it becomes clear that one achieves spiritual integration, not to the extent that one follows the rules of some particular religion or other, but to the extent that one makes peace with oneself. The spiritual challenge is to bring into harmony all the facets of one's inner self and one's outer life. When such harmony is increasingly achieved, one grows spiritually—simply because one facet of the self and the master unifying principle is the human spirit.

There is nothing pathological or in any way unhealthy about homosexuality. The bulk of scientific evidence overwhelmingly supports this conclusion. As best we know, sexual orientation depends on a combination of genetic, prenatal hormonal, and early environmental factors. In most cases sexual orientation is certainly set by adolescence and probably by preschool childhood. Homosexuality is a normal variation. So lesbians and gay men will find spiritual enlightenment to the extent that they accept their sexuality and make something positive of it. To the extent that they are in conflict over their homosexuality, their lives and their selves will be fragmented—obviously!—and their personal integration and, therefore, their spiritual growth will be blocked. Obsessed with sex, religions and many societies are so very mistaken about these matters. Here is one clear instance where a scientific understanding of spirituality allows us to criticize religion.

That same conclusion applies to everyone else. In comparison with homosexual people, the situations of bisexual, transgender, transvestite, and intersex people will be even more difficult, more challenging, because our society is so narrow in its understanding of sexuality. Still, one standard holds throughout: spiritual growth depends on one's ability to integrate all the facets of one's particular being. The explanations of spirituality and the techniques that I present in this book are equally applicable to all.

Simplicity

Another aspect of spiritual pursuit is simplicity of life. Pursuit of the spiritual entails increasing detachment from material things. Francis of Assisi may be the Western ideal—or extreme—in this case, yet the other spiritual traditions also have their models of "holy poverty." Mahayana Buddhism, for example, has its bodhisattvas, who beg their day's food each morning and never accept more than they need for that one day.

Once again, insistence on a simple lifestyle is not some killjoy requirement imposed arbitrarily on one's spiritual quest. Profoundly spiritual people find no need for elaborate goods and exotic living accommodations. As people grow spiritually, their preoccupation with material things trails off. Simplicity of lifestyle emerges spontaneously from spiritual integration and is not a negative restriction, but an expression, and an ongoing source, of personal freedom.

In fact, it takes very little to sustain a healthy, physical life, and people who are also psychologically healthy require a minimum of creature comforts. They find life's fulfillment simply in the living. As Jesus phrased the matter, "Do not worry about your life, what you will eat or what you will drink, or about your body, what you will wear. Is not life more than food, and the body more than clothing?" (Matthew 6:25). Abraham Maslow's description of self-actualizing people exemplifies the matter. According to Maslow, highly integrated people show simplicity and naturalness, and lack artificiality. They are problem-centered, not ego-centered; that is, they're concerned to address the issues, not to make themselves look good. More than others, they enjoy solitude and privacy. They maintain serenity in situations that would drive others to despair.

In the last analysis, however, the measure of simplicity is not the number of a person's possessions, but the sense of detachment with which a person keeps and uses possessions. Of course, a person who is truly detached is not likely to have a store of possessions beyond what is needed for his or her life and work. So the seductive line of some contemporary gurus is grossly misleading, that one can pursue wealth and opulence and still be spiritually advanced. A wealthy person can achieve profound spirituality, but a profoundly spiritual person is unlikely to be concerned about wealth. Again, as Jesus phrased the matter, "It is easier for a camel to pass through the eye of a needle than for a rich person to enter the kingdom of God" (Mark 10:25). A spiritually advanced person is not likely to deal in wealth—except to use it wisely and generously for the good of all!

Social Interaction

On many levels the spiritual person is connected to other people. It is a myth that profound spirituality requires that one be a hermit. I already noted how silence, the avoidance of interaction with people, can facilitate spiritual integration. Sometimes it is useful to abstract oneself from the hurly-burly of social life. But a deliberate campaign of social isolation can be a self-destructive, neurotic, defensive maneuver. It hides one from the natural demands of social and political involvement and deprives one of the emotional growth that intimacy provokes. People become hermits for the sake of later returning to the tribe. This theme of withdrawal and return is constant throughout the spiritual traditions. So much is this the case that Arnold Toynbee names this process a key factor in the development of civilization: certain creative people spend time pursuing the meaning of life and then enrich us all by returning to share their wisdom. To be spiritual does not mean to be isolated.

While on the spiritual path, it is imperative to have others with whom to consult and with whom to share one's experiences. Touching base periodically with a spiritual friend or advisor or with kindred spirits helps keep one's spiritual pursuits in perspective. Human contact keeps our feet on the ground. Community is a facet of every religious tradition: temple, ashram, sangha, synagogue, church, mosque.

Carl Jung reported that, while he was going through some intense psychic upheaval, mundane chores like picking up his paycheck helped keep him sane. Isolated and out of touch with others, we tend to "psych out." The literal role of a hermit is austere and dangerous. It is not a path that anyone should casually assume. Moreover, according to Sister Eugene and other wise mentors, there must be more profitable ways to spend one's life than in isolation. Even the true hermit must at some point return to the marketplace. Otherwise, what value is the desert experience? How truly spiritual could a person be who lives always in his or her own individual world?

To be profoundly spiritual is to identify with all others at a profound level. Through spiritual pursuit we find ourselves; we become ever more securely our unique, individual selves. The more we integrate our spiritual capacity, however, the more surely we identify with all others who share the human spirit. In the depths of our own hearts and souls we find the common humanity that unites us all. The more surely we become ourselves, the more deeply we identify with others. Increased individuality results in increased sociality. For this reason all the spiritual traditions link spiritual growth with concern for others. Once again, the commandment to love is not an arbitrary requirement imposed from outside—it grows directly out of the depths of the human heart. As the Buddhist tradition phrases the matter, compassion in the human heart is like the beautiful lotus that springs up out of the muck of a swamp. And the Jewish prophet Micah (6:8) summarized true spirituality as follows: "What does the Lord require of you but to do justice, to love kindness, and to walk humbly with your God?" Finally, in Christianity, holiness and charity are virtual synonyms, and the same linking occurs in other spiritual traditions.

Of course, the more integrated a person becomes, the fewer kindred spirits she or he will likely encounter—and especially in a materialistic, superficial society like our own. Thus, it may well be that a spiritual adept will appear to be a hermit, a misfit, "a voice crying in the wilderness" (as John the Baptist described himself), and the burden of loneliness may be great. To some extent, personal integrity always carries a price, and isolation may be part of it. Our society does not support those who pursue true spirituality. Nonetheless, social isolation is not characteristic of the spiritual path per se. Somewhere, somehow one can and must find kindred spirits, and, as spiritual commitment more and more becomes a necessity of life, kindred spirits on the path will abound.

In today's world a viable understanding of spirituality must cut across religious traditions and apply to all humanity equally. Such an understanding will foster more widespread spiritual commitment. Thus, this book goes on to elaborate such an understanding of spirituality.

PART TWO

The Psychology
of Spirituality

CHAPTER 9

The Human Spirit

I GOT MY DRIVER'S LICENSE when I was sixteen. My dad taught me to drive. I am still amazed at his patience as I was learning parallel parking, and then learning to start and stop on a steep hill. This latter skill is essential in hilly Pittsburgh, and, since we were driving a car with a standard transmission, negotiating those hills was a challenge. One evening my dad took me to a local warehouse that had a steep incline for an entrance ramp. Halfway up that ramp, I started and stopped again and again until I could perform the operation effortlessly. Simultaneously and in one smooth movement—gas the engine, engage the clutch, and release the handbrake. Learning took practice. Only by repeatedly doing as I was instructed did I learn to drive.

Going Deeper

Not only did my dad tell me what to do and give me ample practice doing it; he also explained how the car works and why I was doing what I did. He explained that the clutch connects two sets of gears, one from the engine and another from the wheels. These gears are moving at different speeds. I had to learn to use the gas pedal to synchronize the speed of the gears so that they could mesh smoothly when I engaged the clutch. My dad also explained that the gears are of different sizes, so shifting from first gear to second, third, and fourth effects a trade-off of power for speed. The lower gears provide more power but are limited in speed. In the lower gears many rotations of the engine effect only one rotation of the wheels, so the wheels have a lot of power, the "condensed" power of the engine's many turns. Since I had studied pulleys, levers, and gears in my high-school science class, I easily understood my dad's explanation.

Understanding helped me drive better. I see the difference in some of my friends who know only how to follow the instructions they were given. They shift thoughtlessly through the gears in a habitual sequence without any concern for being on level ground or on a hill. They don't seem to realize that a car cannot efficiently climb hills in the higher gears. Acting on merely rote learning, they don't really understand what they are doing.

Yet I want to insist that this wondrous marvel is ourselves, nothing more, nothing divine, nothing other-worldly.

My belief has always been that you can do something better if, more than just following a set of instructions, you actually understand what you're up to. What applies to driving a car also applies to doing meditation. In part 1 of this book, I gave instructions and helpful hits for the practice of meditation. Here I am presenting a psychological explanation of spiritual growth, and I presume that this understanding will help you, my reader, in your practice of meditation and in your own spiritual quest.

My lifelong quest for spiritual understanding brought me to this conclusion: certain mental exercises and lifestyles can gradually restructure a person's psyche. Then the inherent spiritual capacity within the human mind can more and more take the lead. This process of human integration is the sum and sub-stance of spiritual growth—and mental health. The key to understanding this process is to recognize that the human mind is twofold: the mind includes both psyche and spirit. I already introduced these notions in chapter 2, and now I go into detail.

"Merely" Human

At the outset, I insist again that the spirit is something fully and "simply" human. It is not God inside us or some "spark of divinity" or a sharing in a cosmic mind or any such theological or metaphysical reality. It is simply a dimension of the human mind, a built-in capacity, a distinctive characteristic of human-ity. Commonly we speak of human awareness, intelligence, or free choice. These are all aspects or expressions of the human spirit. These aspects are certainly marvelous. They open us up to a universe of wonder and, in some way, allow us even to iden-tify with, to take in, or to become that universe. Yet it is clear that the capacity to do so is our very own; it is what makes us human. And even as we do somehow "take in" the universe, or at least parts of it, it is clear that we ourselves are not the uni-verse and, even more so, that we ourselves are not the source of it: we are not God, nor is the depth of our mind. The human spirit is an aspect of our own selves; it is "only" a marvelous capacity of our human minds. It is what allows us to be aware of ourselves as somebody, to claim a specific identity. It is what gives every person worth and inalienable dignity; it makes every person invaluable. Yet it remains "merely" human.

I put quotes around *simply*, *only*, and *merely* because, obvi-ously, I am speaking of something wondrous and uncontain-able. Yet I want to insist that this wondrous marvel *is* ourselves, nothing more, nothing divine, nothing other-worldly. The problem is that none of us is ordinary; every human being, every soul (to use pastoral language) is a remarkable and extra-ordinary reality. Yet the human, wondrous as it is, though potentially open to everything, is not everything: it is simply, only, merely itself. Widespread spiritual talk wants to make the human into more, and suggestions that we are divine have become commonplace. I reject this identification of the human with God in whatever form, subtle or overt. I believe that this confusion of the spiritual with the divine is the root of much confusion about spirituality.

The spiritual aspect of our humanity is empirically verifiable: we can experience it. You don't have to take my word about the spiritual, and I don't have to appeal to revelation or special giftedness or some metaphysical source to confirm my assertions. What I speak of is not religious, nor dependent on faith. What I speak of is within us, and anyone who cares to do so can attend to it. Moreover, once aware of it, we can analyze, describe, and detail this aspect of our being. This very analysis was the major contribution of Bernard Lonergan and, in another form, is also at the heart of Buddhism. And what Lonergan formulated and what I am describing here, you, my reader, can recognize in your own self.

We tend to underestimate our own self-transcending nature, and, on the other hand, we tend to confuse the spiritual with the divine. As a result, we do not acknowledge our own inherent spiritual capacity, and we fail to truly recognize the dimensions of the Ultimate Mystery that we name God. As this final assertion makes clear, my intent is not to deny God, but to reclaim a proper and defensible basis for talk of God. Part 3 of this book addresses this theological matter in detail.

Experiencing Spirit

Most immediately, we experience spirit as our own sense of wonder, marvel, awe. Because of such awe, we stand "outside ourselves." We are bigger than we can say. We include more than we imagine. But to make my point again, this "more" is ourselves. *We* include that "outside." The bigness is what we are. And to be seemingly outside ourselves is to be precisely what we are. We are openness to the universe.

Standing in awe, we are aware, and we are self-aware. Such dual awareness is at the heart of wonder and marvel and awe. We are aware of something that confronts us, and, at the same time but in another mode, we are also aware of ourselves, aware of our own awareness of that something. Thus, we experience a distance between ourselves and that something. This experienced distance, this discrepancy between what we are and what we are now encountering, is the space in which wonder and awe arise. The wonder is the awareness that there is something there, something that, to some extent, we already do know insofar as we are, indeed, aware of it; yet, since it is something new, we really don't know it. So we are taken by this distance. We experience wonder, marvel, awe. Observing children explore their world, one can almost see on their faces the internal phenomenon that I am describing. Children stop in their tracks when they encounter novelty. They radiate a quizzical wonder as they are taken with something new.

From Awe to Questioning and Knowing

Being aware and in wonder, we begin to ask questions. Or, said more accurately, questions arise in us. Out of our wonder and awe, our very being generates questions. We want further understanding. Such spontaneous questioning—spontaneous unless we start memorizing answers or "taking things on faith" or become jaded to life—points us beyond ourselves. Our very being is out-going. There is within us a dynamic force that moves us ever beyond ourselves. This force is our human spirit.

> The little girl would not be suppressed. At one point when
> a particularly stunning firework exploded high overhead,
> she gasped at the top of her shrill, girly voice, "Mommy,
> mommy, I want to shoot up into the sky and pop!"

With questions, insights eventually emerge. We understand. We move beyond our former selves. We reach out into broader reality. But our very being, reaching for reality, wanting to embrace the universe, is not satisfied with mere insights, mere understanding—because we might be wrong. So our own spontaneous outgoing nature pushes us to question now in a new mode. We want to know if our ideas are right, so we check them out. This checking out is not the same process as our original awareness nor as our original questioning and tentative understanding. This checking out is yet another phase of our spiritual unfolding, and it leads us with surety into reality, so we are able to say, "Yes, it is so," or "No, I was mistaken."

From Knowing to Doing

Then our yes or no prompts our outgoing being into yet another mode of operation. All of a piece, and sometimes despite ourselves, our very being urges us to ponder the implications of our knowing, and we are moved to convert that knowing into doing. We have a built-in need to walk our talk. Our human nature pressures us to live with integrity—that is, with consistency or harmony both within ourselves and with our world. Our being urges us to act on our knowledge, to go out of ourselves, to decide, to choose, to commit and engage ourselves, to value, to prize, to love. Step by step we move into the universe. On a track of ever-expanding awareness, understanding, knowledge, and choice, we become one with all that is. Our selves and our world coincide.

I have described the human spirit in some rather ordinary ways: awareness, questions, answers, verifications, and decisions about life in the world. Those who see in the human intellect only rationality and logic might say that I'm not talking about expansive and elusive spirit at all but, rather, some narrowly conceived, deductive function of the mind. Yet I also spoke of an open-ended process that, through awareness, insight, and love, leads us to become one with the universe. Clearly, I am not speaking of a "logic-ing," mechanistic, rationalistic mind, but of an aspect of the mind that does, indeed, show itself in logic and rationality but also in a dynamism that transcends logic and deductive reasoning. Insight makes leaps that leave logic lagging behind, and "the heart has reasons that reason does not know" (as Blaise Pascal noted).

Spirit at Play

My most delightful recognition of human spirit was at a Fourth of July fireworks display on the mall in Washington, D.C. A young family stood nearby as people oohed and aahed. Inconceivably, the parents tried to hush their two children so as "not to disturb people." The little girl would not be suppressed. At one point when a particularly stunning firework exploded high overhead, she gasped at the top of her shrill, girly voice, "Mommy, mommy, I want to shoot up into the sky and pop!"

In that comment I heard not just childish delight, but, despite a sad parental attempt to squash it, the self-transcending human spirit expressing itself. Taken up with the stunning beauty of the moment, this six-year-old went out of herself in embrace of that magic. Far from standing aloof in distant, objective observation to categorize, analyze, and theorize about the data, she fully identified with her experience of the firework, the marvel of which she was a part and which was a part of her. She wanted somehow even more intensely to become the firework itself. Hers was a moment of self-transcendence, a moment of ecstasy. Hers was, if you will, a moment of mystical union. Such is the reality and the capacity of the human spirit—until we stamp it down, train and socialize it, box it into manageable categories, lose sight of all its marvel, conceive it as "mere" rationality, and then lament that we have lost our sense of the spiritual and go looking for it in some land of religious and metaphysical speculation.

So what is spirit? An innate, self-transcending capacity that energizes the human being. Well, then, is spirit an energy? Is it an entity? Is it a link to another world? Depending on how you set up your philosophical analysis, spirit could be said to be all three, and it could also be said to be none of these. But before saying anything, one would have to explain what "energy" means, and "entity," "world," and "another world." And how many bother to precisely define their terms before going on to use them to explain other similarly subtle things like spirit?

Spirit is, indeed, an energy insofar as it moves and urges us. It is an entity insofar as we can affirm that it really does exist; it is something we can name and describe. And it does link us with another world insofar as its self-transcending operation keeps breaking down our current, petty world and opening us up to something new and unexpected. Yet, on the other hand, spirit is our very own being, or at least an aspect of it, and we are not energy but human beings, so in this regard spirit is not an energy—although with Einstein one could insist that we, or at least our physical components, are fully convertible to energy.

Or again, if we can correctly affirm that spirit does exist, it is, nonetheless, not an entity other than ourselves. It does not exist in itself; it exists as one dimension that explains our own being as human. Finally, the ever-new world to which spirit's functioning opens us is not some realm other than our very own, not some additional metaphysical or spiritual world or a parallel universe to which we can go to escape our reality; we are open to the whole of reality, and all reality is one. There is but one world, one universe.

Discussion of these matters is both subtle and complex. The pithy responses I give only open onto still more questions, which we could pursue.

I am aware of the fascinating questions that perk in spiritual circles. However, these questions no longer entice me. Most of them depend on complex misconceptions, which can be resolved by hard-won, clear thinking. But the clear thinking brings us right back down to earth to face the life that is ours. Thus, I see little value in pursuing such metaphysical speculation, and certainly I do not wish to do so in this book. While we speculate about an imagined and, thus, ultimately unknowable realm, our life in the real world is seeping away. Better to bite the bullet, better to take up the reins, and begin living alertly right here and now. Such living is precisely what all the spiritual traditions advocate. The following chapter will take us more deeply into the inner structures of our this-worldly living.

CHAPTER 10

The Dynamics of Spiritual Growth

∞

ADOLESCENTS ARE OFTEN CLUMSY, but the clumsiness is not their fault. Their bodies are growing fast and, what is more, unevenly. Parts of the body farthest from the trunk develop first, so for a while adolescents have disproportionately big hands and feet and long arms and legs. Understandably, they often trip over themselves. Eventually that awkward period passes, and the adolescents become young women and men. They look fine, and they are poised and in control. Their bodies have reached a point of balance and harmony.

Growth in spirituality advances in a similar way. Different facets of a person—body, psyche, and spirit—have their own needs and inclinations, so together they function in a shifting tension, tugging now in this direction and pulling now in that. The goal is to get all three to function harmoniously. On the way to that goal, we are likely to experience some awkwardness. However, unlike in physical maturation, which is complete in a couple of years, spiritual growth goes on in some form our whole life through. Still, all spiritual growth involves the same basic process. This chapter describes the core process of spiritual growth.

The key to understanding spirituality is the human spirit. It is an innate, open-ended, outgoing, dynamic dimension of the human mind. Our spiritual capacity leads us ever beyond ourselves as we become that beyond that opens onto the universe. The human spirit is the innate basis of all spiritual pursuit.

But spirit is not the only dimension of the human mind. Spirit is not even the most obvious dimension. Its subtlety explains the fact that spirit is often overlooked when we talk about the mind, and the pervasiveness of its working leads us to take spirit for granted and to leave it unnamed. Other aspects of mind are more dominant.

Three Other Facets of the Mind

Emotions come upon us and sometimes bowl us over. Even people who are rather unfeeling know what anger, sadness, fear, and excitement are. And people who are more sensitive can report an array of subtle feelings, passing responses to particular events as well as many different, ongoing, and sometimes quite passionate emotional states.

Mental imagery is another obvious facet of the mind. Even people who say they never dream can remember at least one dream, so they can say what a mental image is. Besides, all of us use mental images to think and plan and strategize; our fantasy life is filled with images; and images come to mind as part of our memories.

Memories make up another category of mental phenomena that are very well known to everyone. Memories can come upon us unexpectedly. At other times we deliberately pull up memories and use this stored information for our daily tasks. Indeed, it is memory that keeps us aware of ourselves and our doings. The movie *Memento* powerfully illustrated the effects of loss of memory and so, the importance of memory in our everyday lives.

These facets of the mind—emotions, imagery, and memory—work together and are intertwined. A memory will often emerge in imaginative form and will bring with it a flood of feelings. For example, as soon as I think of the Scots College in Rome, I can picture in my mind the building, the playing fields, and the corridors and rooms, and with each image comes a scene filled with varying emotions.

These facets of the mind working together make us who we are. Our biography, embodied in our very being, is a composite of memories, emotions, and images. In large part, these determine our personalities, our habitual ways of behaving and reacting. Shy or outgoing, energetic or sluggish, circumspect or trusting, in touch or spaced out, inquisitive or bored, affirming or berating, social or solitary—these characteristics are built into us. Our living builds them in; our past experiences program us for further experience.

These mental programs, our personalities, are the structures through which we experience our worlds and through which we shape our worlds. And these two, the experiencing and the shaping, go hand in hand. They work together toward a balance, a consistency. For this reason, we fall into routines, and we repeatedly have the same kind of experiences, good as well as bad. For example, how many people do you know who consistently fall in love with the same kind of losers? And how many people do you know who amazingly somehow find a way to land on their feet after any bad tumble in life? As they say, we are creatures of habit.

If we are mentally healthy, the structures of our mind are stable. We exhibit a certain consistency, a predictability in our reactions and behaviors. People can recognize us to be ourselves and sometimes comment that we are not being ourselves. Yet these structures are not permanent. They can be changed. We can develop a sense of humor, we can learn to be more sensitive to others, we can outgrow a semidepressed state of mind.

Psyche and Spirit

I speak of these inner structures of our experience as *psyche*. Different psychologists use this term in different ways. I mean by it what I just described: the conglomerate of memories, images, and emotions that together form our personalities and structure our experience.

Psyche is a stabilizing factor of the mind; psyche tends to support the status quo. In contrast, spirit is the dynamic factor in the mind; as a self-transcending force within us, spirit tends to novelty, change, growth. Growth occurs as the structures of the psyche shift and reconfigure. Many things can effect such a shift. As it unfolds, life itself inevitably brings surprises that challenge us and force change upon us. We change to survive. Intimate relationships—and especially falling in love—are particularly powerful in shaking up our inner lives and opening us to new experiences. Sometimes we deliberately pursue change when we decide to break bad habits and work to develop needed character traits. Sometimes we enlist professional help, such as counseling, to effect such change.

We fall into routines, and we repeatedly have the same kind of experiences, good as well as bad. How many people do you know who consistently fall in love with the same kind of losers?

If the change we experience is positive, it attunes us more and more fully to the internal influence of our open-ended, dynamic, self-transcending spiritual capacity. In this case, we speak of the change as personal growth. Still, negative, limiting, restrictive changes are also possible. As life unfolds, people sometimes stagnate, shut down, go sour; they become hardened in their narrow and petty ways. Burdensome routines some-times wear away at people until they grow weary and become dull. And for the sake of short-term gains, people sometimes deliberately choose dishonest and selfish—and ultimately lim-iting—ways, which become standard practice for them. But when change is positive, it involves opening to one's own human spirit. Indeed, openness to the spirit is what defines what is *positive*. Our human spirit is an unbounded dynamism within us; it expresses the movement of life in its subtlest form and tends toward a unifying embrace of all that is. Thus, ever-increasing welcome to our self-transcending spirit is the essen-tial meaning of growth, health, and positive change.

By the same token, such positive change and personal growth are the very meaning of spiritual development. Insofar as such change depends on openness to one's spirit and insofar as growth represents increasing integration of one's spiritual capacity, personal growth *is* spiritual growth. Its mechanism is the shifting of the structures of the psyche, and its essence is the integration of the spirit.

All approaches to personal growth, deliberate or imposed, depend on this same mechanism and express this same essen-tial. To this extent, contentless meditation can be a universal lubricant. It can help smooth out the awkward times of spiri-tual growth. Meditation can facilitate personal growth no mat-ter how growth is being pursued or provoked in any particular case. Meditation is an exercise in focused openness to the spirit, so meditation makes any human experience more profound and, at the same time, more transforming. The next three chap-ters detail the positive effects of meditation and show how far-reaching these effects can be.

CHAPTER 11

Immediate Effects of Meditation

∞

A S WE SAW IN THE PREVIOUS CHAPTER the mechanism of positive, personal change—that is, spiritual growth—is the shifting of the psyche that allows the increasing dominance of the spirit. Meditation facilitates such growth by deliberately engaging this mechanism. Meditation strengthens the subtle urgings of the human spirit by giving them more room. Then the dynamism of the spirit can overcome the stagnation of the psyche, a gentle shake-up can occur, and facets of the psyche can realign themselves in ways more congenial to the openness of the spirit. During meditation, locked-up emotions, memories, and images are released so that, under the benign and gracious unifying influence of the spirit, the psyche can reconfigure itself in a healthier form.

It is possible to describe the specific effects of meditation in some detail. I present such a description below. Our discussion moves from the most common to the most subtle and rare effects, but the process in any particular case won't necessarily move exactly in the order discussed here. This description should be taken as a helpful guide, not as the fixed and invariant pattern.

Relaxing and De-stressing

The most common effect of meditation is relaxation. So much is this the case that, viewing meditation with the eyes of a medical doctor, Herbert Benson named his book on meditation *The Relaxation Response*. Of course, finding a way to relax could be a supreme good for some people and a benefit to all of us, yet relaxation is only a first and a superficial effect of meditation.

With physiological measures, studies have documented relaxation. Meditation reduces the rate of metabolism in the body. Within three minutes of beginning meditation, a 10 to 20 percent decrease in consumption of oxygen is noticeable. Simultaneously, heart and breathing rates decrease. EEG readings—a measure of electrical activity in the brain—show a shift to the healthy alpha range, which indicates a mental state between waking awareness and sleep. In addition, levels of lactate in the blood (an indicator of stress) decrease, and blood pressure decreases. These latter effects remain constant between meditation periods if a person meditates regularly. No wonder health professionals encourage people to meditate!

A related effect of relaxation is what some have called "unstressing." It is the spontaneous release of physical tensions carried in the body. During meditation people may experience twitches, spasms, gasps, tingling, jerking, swaying, aches, pressures. Sometimes uncontrollable laughter or unexplained weeping results. It seems that the body spontaneously releases pent up tension when we relax—as when we startle and jerk on the brink of falling asleep—and this release shows in these physiological effects.

Some people theorize that for years and decades we might "carry" the tensions—the hurts and pains—of life in various parts of our bodies, and these burdensome tensions partially explain things like backaches, stomach problems, foot and leg pains, and the like. Supposedly, when allowed, the body will spontaneously release this unhealthy tension and realign itself in a more comfortable and balanced configuration. This realignment of the body would seem to be a physical parallel to the realignment of the psyche, described in chapter 10: under the lead of the spirit, our whole being tends toward balance, wholeness, and integration.

That such realignment of the body is an effect of meditation was noted in the medieval spiritual classic *The Cloud of Unknowing*. Its anonymous author reported that monks who meditated regularly appeared young, physically balanced, and attractive well into their elder years. In addition to the health benefit of relaxation, this promise of good looks could provide our vain culture with yet another motivation for regular meditation.

Desensitization

A more internal effect of meditation is akin to a process called "systematic desensitization." Psychologist Joseph Wolpe developed this process to help people overcome anxieties and phobias. In a relaxed state, a patient is asked to confront a list of stressors, working his or her way from the least to the most distressing. Since, supposedly, relaxation and tension are incompatible, led through this list, step by step, the patient learns to face increasingly disturbing situations without the anxiety or fear that they usually provoke. Thus, the patient is systematically desensitized to anxiety-producing stressors and is eventually freed from her or his phobias.

Similarly, during meditation one enters a state of deep relaxation. At the same time disturbing issues in one's mind will eventually show themselves in the form of thoughts, memories, images, and emotions. In accord with the meditation technique, one acknowledges these inner productions and gently dismisses them. One practices being indifferent to whatever arises in the mind, so disturbing things eventually become just other passing thoughts. Over a period of time, confronted again and again, these concerns gradually lose their power. Regular meditation thus has the potential to free one from worries and preoccupations.

Relation to Psychotherapy

Notice that this process parallels psychotherapy. In the counselor's office, in an environment of welcome and trust, one is gradually able to reveal one's deepest and darkest secrets. Facing them in the light of day defuses their power, and somehow one finds oneself released from long-standing emotional burdens.

***

Neurotic saints used to be acceptable, but no more.
Today we know better, so we are not free to plead blissful
ignorance and cast responsibility onto God or the devil.
They get blamed for so much in this world!

***

On this score, two points need to be made. First, as a parallel to psychotherapy, meditation should be taken seriously as a powerful tool. Second, nonetheless, meditation is not a substitute for psychotherapy when a person is dealing with serious psychological issues. Sometimes we do need professional help to loosen the impacted psyche and free us from the paralyzing effects of past traumas and their deeply ingrained, counterproductive patterns of behavior. Meditation can be a help in the healing process, but by itself meditation is not the prescribed cure.

There is a difference between deep psychic healing through psychotherapy and the more subtle "polishing" of a basically healthy psyche through meditation. Ignorance of this difference results in the contradiction of a person well versed in spiritual lore and even experienced in spiritual subtleties but, nonetheless, as kooky as all get out.

Unaware of psychodynamics—that is, the inner workings of the mind—that old-time religion turned to expected prayer, repentance, and resolve to cure every ill. But in most cases there was no cure, just a deceptive form of rigidly determined willpower and dangerously intense religious commitment. Still ignoring psychodynamics, current spiritual movements may likewise promise bliss and prosperity while ignoring adherents' blatant neuroses, so we often find some very eccentric people among spiritual "groupies." In the past the neurotic saint may have been an acceptable phenomenon. Think of Blessed Pierre de Luxembourg, who was so scrupulous that he had a priest ever by his side so he could confess his sins on demand; Hildegard of Bingen, whose mystical "visions" match the hallucinations symptomatic of oncoming migraine headaches; Saint Teresa of Avila, whose "raptures" were apparently caused by neurological seizures; or Muhammad, the Prophet of Islam, whose strange spells would fit the diagnosis for temporal lobe epilepsy. Neurotic saints used to be acceptable, but no more. Today we know better, so we are not free to plead blissful ignorance and cast responsibility onto God or the devil. They get blamed for so much in this world!

On the other hand, that spiritual leaders may have suffered from mental disturbances does not diminish their greatness. They were able to use their peculiar, distressing, and often painful experiences to gain insight and become better people. They grew through their afflictions. Surely, for example, Teresa of Avila's struggle with neuropathology forced her to learn to ignore the noises she heard in her head and to give attention to her healthy, deeper core—just as one is to do during meditation practice: let go of thoughts, images, and emotions that arise, and return to one's word. Despite and even because of the mental burdens they carried, these historical figures have made major contributions to culture and religion. It is because of these contributions that these people stand among the greats, not because of their "visions," "raptures," and "spells." We need to be careful to get the lesson right.

We must not assume that spiritual practice itself will treat our neuroses. The failure to properly treat deep psychopathology explains why some regular meditators eventually come up against a brick wall in their spiritual journey. The gentle healing that meditation can effect goes only so far. Meditation best opens a path to profound spiritual growth for people who already enjoy basic psychological health.

In fact, meditation may not be useful at all, but actually destructive, to people dealing with severe mental illness. Meditation works by gradually loosening the fossilized structures of the psyche, but people with mental illness need stability. For the most part, they cannot afford to tamper with their psyches, so, sad to say, they must often be satisfied with a less than cheerful mental state and a colorless spiritual life.

It is important to recognize that people are not all equally gifted or blessed. In one way or another, all of us labor under liabilities and personal inadequacies, some of them virtually insurmountable. We must do the best with what we have. For whatever reason of nature or nurture, some people are simply incapable of profound, cultivated spiritual awareness. They can, nonetheless, meet the down-to-earth spiritual ideal that I am presenting throughout this book. The spiritual call for all of us is one and the same, to live as alertly as we are able and as responsibly as our situation demands. As each of us meets the level of personal integration of which we are capable, in some way we all fulfill the one human call to be responsible citizens of our world. Achievement of extraordinary spiritual experiences is not the criterion of spiritual fulfillment. So, to my mind, each in his or her own way is capable of spiritual fulfillment, but those ways differ. As Jesus phrased the matter, from those to whom more has been given, more is required. Only some will be capable of subtle spiritual awareness, and part of the "more" to which they are called is to take up the slack for those who have received less.

The next chapter describes even further effects of regular meditation.

CHAPTER 12

Far-reaching Effects of Meditation

∞

As we discussed, meditation easily induces a healthy state of deep relaxation. Within that state the body may release tension through twitches, jerks, groans, and other spontaneous behaviors, and the mind gradually becomes desensitized to anxious and fearful thoughts.

The meditative effect that I have called desensitization affects aspects of the mind that lie near the surface. But consistent meditation has a further and more profound effect. Meditation can also provoke the release of ghosts and goblins that lie hidden in the caverns of the psyche—deeply repressed psychodynamic material.

During meditation an array of monsters tend at times to assault people—memories, thoughts, feelings, and images that are grotesque, disgusting, violent, or lewd. At this point in the process, especially if intensely pursued, some meditators become fearful of their own minds and complain that they are "going crazy."

Such experiences can be part and parcel of ongoing meditative practice. One theory suggests that the mind needs something to keep it busy, and when outside stimuli are minimized—as in an isolation tank or as when one does nothing but sit still and internally repeat a word—the mind itself will produce content to "entertain" itself. As in dreams, that content will be a sometimes bizarre creation made up from disparate elements of one's history and one's fantasies.

During meditation, these emergences, like any other, should simply be acknowledged and gently dismissed. Because of the hypnotic-like ritual of meditation, the emotional charge of mental experience during meditation tends to be relatively low. Thus, one can tolerate even such disturbing mental productions without really "losing one's mind." Still, this discussion should be a reminder that the spiritual path is not all fun and games. People who pursue the purification and restructuring of their minds should expect to encounter disgusting things. A popular saying relates to these matters: "You have to get your s--t together." Dealing with such stuff is bound to be messy.

The Restructured World

That process of cleaning out one's deeper mind is a matter of the personal unconscious; it pertains to an aspect of mind that is unique to each one of us. A still further effect of consistent meditation regards the world that we share in common; long-practiced meditation also restructures the socially constructed world.

The world in which we actually live is not some ready-made, passively accepted affair. It is a construct. Individually, we all construct a personal world for ourselves, so we can say of tragic occasions, "My world came tumbling down." But we also inherit or buy into a world constructed by society. This world shared with others can also be shaken, and millions might experience its tottering—as, for example, when two hijacked planes crashed into the World Trade Center and led observers to report that "the psyche of America was assaulted" and "our world will never be the same."

Things that we take for granted, things we believe to be hard-wired into reality, turn out to be of our own making—and they can be unmade. Supposedly, Eskimo peoples have many words for snow. The highly nuanced experience of winter that they know must be different from ours. Likewise, much Asian music makes use of sounds that fall between the cracks of our piano keys. As a result, what our ears are likely to hear is different from what Asians experience. We live in different worlds; our worlds are constructed differently. Consistent meditation can break down these constructions of reality and leave us facing the raw and unstructured data, devoid of coherence or meaning, that go into such constructions. In this case, the world can literally dissolve before our eyes.

Distancing

The meditative exercise—simply observing and gently letting go of every perception, thought, image, emotion, or memory that arises—distances us from all these contents of our minds. We stand apart from them. We dis-identify with them. Gradually we come to experience that we are not all that. Our thoughts and perceptions, our very experiences of "reality," occur in our minds. They are all "just thoughts," "just feelings," "just perceptions," all equally relevant and equally irrelevant. This exercise levels our inner experience, makes everything of equal import. As a result, we can be open to all incoming experience equally. We can be receptive to aspects of possible experience that we—and our society—may generally overlook. We can integrate experience and reintegrate it in novel ways. Nothing need be set in concrete as a result of our prefabricated conceptual frameworks. We are not locked into our understanding of things. We can reconfigure our experience of "the world" and in the process create and know a different world. We are free to experience things differently.

I speak of "we" reintegrating or reconfiguring our experience, yet the process is a spontaneous one. It is, indeed, each "I"—each one of us in our own right—who does the reconfiguration, but not in any deliberate or calculated way. It is not as if my conscious "I" is in charge. By this point in the meditative experience, we have learned well to just let things be as we actively yet unintrusively observe them: any and every mental happening is all just thought, just feeling. So the fascinating and discombobulating experience I am describing unfolds on its own. Some deeper "I" makes the show go on. In a sense that is broader and more integrated than the "I" of my ordinary, self-determined, and contrived living—I do, indeed, create and experience the performance. But gradually my deeper or truer, my more expansive "I" gets to be in charge, and in some sense this "I" functions apart from "me."

Awareness of Mental Constraints

I had a striking example of this kind of experience after days of long hours of practice when I was meditating with the Buddhists in Vermont. The technique I was using allowed for one's eyes to be open. As I sat and looked unfocusedly forward at the wall and window before me, suddenly the window and wall shifted in function, and the window was the opaque surface, and the wall, the opening to the outside. Window and wall lost their meaning, and my mind experienced them in reverse. The experience lasted only an instant because the shock of it pulled me back into my conventional experience of the world. Yet in that moment it was clear to me that my experience of wall and window depended heavily on my learning to experience and categorize things in that specific configuration. In fact, the genius of a developmental psychologist, Jean Piaget, elaborated the process of how infants actually learn to conceptualize the physical world in what he called the sensory-motor stage of cognitive development. What I experienced was the momentary breakdown of that early learning.

Obviously, that breakdown could go even further, and one would not even experience wall and window in any interrelationship whatsoever. One would experience only an array of raw data apart from any ordering or configuration. The make-up of the "world" would dissolve completely as unconstrained experience was freed from all conceptual structures. It is toward such an end that meditation practice moves.

What I just described is nothing esoteric. Others know the experience. Most of us have seen the optical illusion that presents a vase or else two faces in silhouette looking at each other. What one sees while looking at this presentation depends on how one happens to perceive the thing, and the perception changes as figure and ground shift. Background becomes foreground or vice versa, and what looked like a vase now looks like two faces or vice versa.

The Validity of Constructs

The peculiarity of that optical illusion is that it is deliberately contrived. The perceptual data are purposefully ambiguous so that one can perceive either a vase or two faces, and neither perception can claim to be the correct one. Both are equally correct; both can equally claim grounding in the data. This state of affairs would lead some people to insist that reality is merely an arbitrary construct, that anything could be anything else, and things are merely what we choose to make of them: there is no reality; all things are relative.

I would not jump to conclusions so quickly. The optical illusion and the wall-window experience are of different kinds. Upon reflection, it is clear that there is good reason to distinguish window from wall; these constructs do have valid significance in the real world. Although we are capable of deprogramming our constructions, an understanding of this capacity does not imply that our constructions are all invalid. Indeed, some constructions are more valid than others, and in some cases multiple constructions may be validly possible. This state of affairs invites us to pursue the most adequate understandings of experience, to construct our world as correctly as possible. This state of affairs does not imply that understanding is useless or that all understandings are equally valid.

At stake in this discussion is the belief in truth and in the value of pursuing it. At stake on the opposite pole is the relativism of postmodernism, the rejection of any claim to correct knowledge or objective ethics. I reject this postmodern conceit. Not only does it fly in the face of all the spiritual traditions, it also rests on self-contradiction: while rejecting sure knowledge of any kind, it proposes its rejection as sure knowledge. Misunderstanding and imprecise conceptualization in this subtle area abound. Only these would allow the subversive conclusion that there is no such thing as objective truth. It is a grave misunderstanding of the spiritual traditions to play on these subtleties to support such nonsense. On this score I differ with the metaphysical conclusion of Buddhism—that the world is merely an illusion. Granted, through extensive meditation practice one can actually experience the dissolution of the socially constructed world. However, this experience does not imply that there is no world and that its construction is necessarily mistaken.

Rather than to suppose that the world is an illusion, that reasonable statement has no valid content, and that ethics is a matter of personal taste, regular meditation should lead us to realize that reality is a vast, fascinating, and inviting affair—like fireworks on the Fourth of July. Meditation should lead us to engage our experience and construct reality accordingly—to live, work, and love in a way that ongoingly opens onto the unbounded possibilities of our universe. To do so is to pursue truth and to do good, for creative living with an open-ended future is precisely what these traditional terms imply. The following chapter says more about this ultimate goal of meditation.

CHAPTER 13

Cosmic Consciousness

∽

F OR MANY PEOPLE, the supreme goal of the spiritual
quest is mysticism. But mysticism itself is surrounded by
mystique. People talk of mysticism and even strive to attain it,
but nobody is very sure what the term *mysticism* means. In fact,
it is very difficult to say what mysticism is. This brief chapter
makes an attempt.

As already noted, regular meditation has a set of effects that
range from the ordinary to the unusual. At the far end of this
range is the abiding transformation of a person's mind. Then
one lives with an expanded awareness that can make every ordinary experience profound and marvelous. This achievement
could be called cosmic consciousness, and there are other parallel terms: enlightenment, mysticism, *samadhi*, *satori*, *moksha*,
kensho, and *fana*. Using different terms bearing different connotations, all the spiritual traditions envisage some such state of
purified and expanded awareness.

Through spiritual practice (assisted, where appropriate, with
psychotherapy), one cleanses one's mind of personal biases and
hang-ups and achieves an emotional clarity; one also frees oneself from the collective blinders that cultures supply and
require. Purified, one is open to live in response to the ever-
changing flow of the present moment, experiencing things for

what they are and what they can positively be. One lives free from the limiting presuppositions, known and unconscious, that we tend to bring to our living. The clear mind operates in the present, attending to the here and now. The purified mind is not caught up in fretting about the past or worrying about the future. In this state one responds spontaneously and incisively to what is really going on. One transcends the emotions, sees through the facades, and avoids the social intrigues that so often surround our social interactions.

In this regard I think of the example of Jesus, confronted with "an adulterous woman." His critics challenged him to pronounce judgment, knowing that, if he dismissed her, he would be ignoring the Jewish Law and that, if he condemned her, he would be violating his own call for mercy. He did neither. The scriptures say that he bent down and began to write on the ground. I like to think he was doodling, passing time as he thought and felt this thing through. In touch with himself and also aware of his surroundings, he assessed the situation. He responded by addressing head-on the hypocrisy that lay behind the accusation of the lone woman: "Let the one who is without sin cast the first stone." Thus, he cut to the quick and diffused the situation. He was not caught up in the options presented to him. He saw through to a different construction of reality. He was living in "a different world."

When the meditative state becomes habitual, as Daniel Goleman conceives the matter, it comes to characterize the waking, sleeping, and dreaming states of consciousness. Transforming them all, the meditation-induced state eventually sets up a new, distinct, and enduring state of consciousness: enlightenment or mystical awareness.

Meditation gradually dismantles the structures of the psyche and realigns them. Whereas formerly our thoughts, images, feelings, and memories were programmed to serve our own security and the purposes of society, now our psyche is repro-grammed to serve the open-ended, self-transcending, dynamism of our human spirit. Our personalities become the perfect instruments of the outgoing wonder within us whose ultimate reach is the loving embrace of all that is and can be. With the psyches of educated, experienced, self-structured, and responsible adults, we recover the purity, curiosity, and open-ness of a child. Thus, we become agents of ongoing transfor-mation. We shape ourselves and our world along the lines of open-ended becoming that characterize the really real. Our being and all that is come to coincide. We live at one with the universe in its unending unfolding.

Jesus was not caught up in the options presented to him. He was living in "a different world."

As understood here, the goal of the spiritual quest is not to achieve way-out experiences. It is not to induce altered states of consciousness, to live detached from everyday life, to enjoy blissed-out times of ecstasy, or to be freed from living on this earth and in a physical body. Though an occasional experience of altered consciousness can be spiritually useful—by disrupt-ing everyday awareness, such an experience allows for the wholesome restructuring of the mind—achievement of altered states of consciousness is not the goal of spirituality. Rather, the goal is to live completely down-to-earth and to do so with gusto: to live in the wonder, joy, delight, or poignancy of every moment; to be fully alive, fully alert, fully open to every passing experience; to respond creatively and constructively to every event.

Tony Kushner's *Angels in America* exemplifies this goal. The denouement of the play reveals a vision of an open, diverse, and loving community. There are no angels. There is no Magician God to be found: he has long since been missing from his celestial office. There are only people, friends and lovers, fellow travelers on life's way. Life is not lived in some spiritual realm, distant from everyday life, nor does one expect miraculous help to break in from beyond. For those who have passed through the purifying trials, everyday life is all that is left; but, even in the face of death, when graced by loving companions and open to myriad small beauties, everyday life is not dull and dreary, but wondrous and worthy of praise and filled with gratitude. I imagine the small group of life's pilgrims in the closing scenes of the play to be spiritually enlightened pioneers who are forging a new way of life to replace the magic religions that no longer work. Yet that spiritual community is not without its own magic. The real magic is the wonder, marvel, awe that is already in the human heart.

Meditation is a spiritual practice that gradually transforms a person. Meditation can change our lives. But to do so, meditation must become a part of our lifestyle. Our fast-paced, off-balance, buzzing, and dazzling world has little place for the sanity of regular meditation. Luckily, the practice itself leads to a lifestyle that can center us and, let us hope, reorient our world.

Sex is one of the obsessions that sets our world so much off-balance. The following chapter will look at sex as another practice that can also facilitate spiritual growth.

CHAPTER 14

Sex as a Spiritual Exercise

I N   L I G H T   O F   T H E   H I S T O R Y   of Western civilization, dominated by Christianity, the title of this chapter may seem strange indeed. Christianity affirms the Incarnation, that God actually took on human flesh, and Christianity insists that salvation occurs in and through the Body of Christ. Nonetheless, through the centuries from Christianity's earliest beginnings, in most Christian thinking, the body and the spirit have been seen as enemies to each other.

In its simplest formulation, the teaching of Saint Paul was merely that evil and goodness are at odds. Obviously! But ripped from its cultural context and misunderstood, Paul's actual words in Galatians 5:17 were taken to pit sex against spirituality: "What the flesh desires is opposed to the Spirit, and what the Spirit desires is opposed to the flesh; for these are opposed to each other."

In fact, the sex negativity that has characterized Christianity did not come from Christianity's Jewish heritage, nor from the teachings of Jesus, nor even from the letters of Paul. This negativity came from the secular philosophies that were prevalent during Christianity's formation, especially Stoicism and Neoplatonism. These systems of thought were suspect of pleasure and overly rationalistic. Shortsighted in their appreciation of human sexuality, they argued that sex was for begetting children and that any other use of sex was mistaken. This "mistake" was quickly turned into sin, and into the twenty-first century we all live with the result.

The most brilliant minds of the Christian tradition rationalized that misunderstanding. Saint Augustine is the theological favorite of Protestantism, and Saint Thomas Aquinas is the great theologian of Catholicism. Both understood rationality to be the crowning gift of humanity, and both were wary of sex. At the point of orgasm, they reasoned, one momentarily loses rationality, and the risk of such loss can only be justified for a serious reason. The desire to conceive a child would be the only sufficient reason.

The Positive Aspects of Sex

Augustine and Aquinas were correct: sexual experience does entail a momentary loss of rationality. But with more profound psychological awareness, the wisdom of our age asserts that such a temporary loss might be to the good. The psychoanalytic term that could apply to the matter is "regression in the service of the ego." Sometimes it is useful to suffer a breakdown of our too-heady rationalism. Such breakdown allows our mental structures to regroup in a healthier configuration: one step backward for the sake of two steps forward.

With that notion comes an idea I have emphasized throughout this book. It is sometimes useful to break down our excessively rationalized minds in order to allow our self-transcending spirits to take the lead. Thus, like meditation, sex can also be a path toward personal—and, therefore, spiritual—integration. By moving us out of our prosaic work-a-day worlds and into a more creative mental space, like meditation, sex can foster the transformation of the psyche—which is the practical key to spiritual growth.

Whereas a former age emphasized opposition between body and spirit, contemporary psychological awareness emphasizes integration. Instead of attempting to sequester sex, to restrict, control, and restrain it, our age would let body, psyche, and spirit work in harmonious partnership. Instead of conceiving the spiritual ideal to be emancipation from the physical world and our bodies, our age would find spiritual growth through personal fulfillment in the body. The other-worldly spirituality of a former age is today giving way to a this-worldly spirituality of wholeness and integration. Granted that one facet of human wholeness is spirit, personal integration implies increasing actualization of our spiritual potential. Rather than oppose sex, contemporary emphasis uses sex to elicit the spirit. This effect can occur on two levels: bodily and psychic.

Body

Tibetan Buddhism has long used physical sexual arousal to achieve transcendent experiences. We know this tradition as Tantric sex. In our own society interest in "erotic massage" is popularizing this same approach. It uses full-body massage, including sexual stimulation but without orgasm, to induce intense and prolonged states of physiological arousal. Especially when accompanied by deep-breathing exercises, this arousal can induce profound altered states of consciousness, which facilitate the restructuring of the psyche. Because the body is the foundation of the psyche, any sexual arousal will loosen up the psyche. The relaxation that sexual arousal requires frees up the mind. Fantasy routinely accompanies sexual arousal:

images, memories, and emotions rise up out of the psyche. This shake-up of the psyche opens the way to personal transformation. Thus, sexual arousal can serve as an access to the spirit through the body—just like those other, more standard, body-centered spiritual practices noted in chapter 3.

Psyche

On the level of psyche, although a passing sexual encounter can sometimes be a beneficial experience—the legendary weekend tryst that leaves both parties grateful for one another and restored to faith in life—sexual arousal has its most powerful effect when coupled with romance. From this perspective, it becomes clear that talk at this point is not of casual sex but of ongoing interpersonal relationship. The emotional power of relationships is well known. In some cases it can be explosive, but, to some extent in every case, intimate relationship pries open the psyche. Falling in love and being in love are exciting and disrupting experiences. When people are in love, from their psyches come pouring out memories, joys, and fears—as well as hopes and schemes: the dreams and promises of lovers, the meanings and values, the ideas and ideals, that are the hallmarks of the human spirit. This psychic upheaval turns over rich mental soil and makes way for new growth. With the breakdown of habitual patterns of behavior and response comes the possibility of reconfiguring the self in a healthier form.

Sex can be used to facilitate self-transcending experience. But bringing a purified mind to sex also transforms sex itself. Therefore, compared to the unaware, people who meditate regularly can be more personally engaged in a sexual encounter. They can approach a partner with clarity of focus, knowing why they are there; with intensity of action, being fully present to every touch, movement, and gesture; with emotional attunement, flowing in synch with the partner; with responsiveness of presence, attending spontaneously to the other; and with profound identification, finding themselves in the other and the other in themselves.

Therefore, compared to the unaware, people who meditate regularly can be more personally engaged in a sexual encounter.

At the same time that the regular meditator brings a richer self to the sexual encounter, the bodily and psychic effects of the encounter also further intensify the meditator's personal presence. There is a snowballing effect. Multiple systems conspire to increase personal—and now interpersonal—integration. Bodies, psyches, and spirits flow in the transcending, ever-renewing course that is determined by the open-ended dynamism of spirit itself. A unitive experience—a sense of oneness with oneself, the other, and the universe—may sometimes result. This is to say, in sexual sharing one can know a moment of mystical ecstasy. And this moment helps to further transform the psyche, opening onto the possibility of still further experiences of self-transformation. In this fashion, loving sex can become a path to spiritual fulfillment.

Ideal and Real

However, my down-to-earth sense of life requires that I add a qualification. It must be recalled that most often sex is a rather prosaic event. People usually end up enjoying sex not because it can open the door to mysticism but for this or that more mundane reason. As with spirituality, we must be careful not to idealize sex. It is often less than it is cracked up to be. Sex is, after all, a human affair, and, more often than not, human affairs fall into the gray range, not into black or white.

In any case, sex and spirituality can be integrated. They can mutually enhance one another. Indeed, sex can also be used for escapism; in its own way sex can also become an addiction. It would be a compounded illusion to believe that an insatiable pursuit of sex has spiritual growth as its motive.

The spiritual path follows a fine line. It is the narrow gate of which Jesus spoke, the razor edge that the boddhisatva must walk. If a former age fell off the edge into an other-worldly extreme, advocating a spiritual fulfillment that required the denial of sex, our own age tends to fall off the edge into a this-worldly extreme, ignoring the spiritual and touting the value of physical comfort and pleasure. Finding and expressing a balance is not easy to do. But worse than missing the balance is to not even attempt to find it. Integration of sexuality and spirituality may call for some experimentation, and along the way one may make some mistakes. One only hopes that we all have the good sense not to make irreparable mistakes—like unwanted pregnancies, incurable sexually transmitted diseases, broken hearts, or scandalous betrayals of solemn commitments. I treat the integration of sexuality and spirituality in detail in my book *Sex and the Sacred.*

Spirituality is a quest. Composed of body, psyche, and spirit, we live pulled in many directions. The challenge each day is to pursue a new balance as life inevitably changes and moves on. The key to the balance is attunement to our own spirit, for the spirit holds a fountain of wisdom that is beyond our deliberate control.

For that very reason—because our own spirit seems to operate from beyond ourselves, because our spirit certainly is more than our small, conceptualized selves—people tend to attribute spiritual experiences to things outside of themselves, most commonly, to "God." The concluding chapters of this book delve into that matter both to sort out and to interrelate the spiritual and the divine.

PART THREE

God, Religion, and Spirituality

CHAPTER 15

Spirituality without God?

∞

THIS BOOK HAS BEEN EXPLAINING the nuts and bolts of the spiritual quest. When I began my spiritual quest as a naïve adolescent, I did not really understand what spiritual growth was all about. Neither, it seemed to me, did anyone else. Through the years I came to make better sense of the matter, and in this book I have shared this basic insight: spiritual growth is nothing other than ongoing human integration. My seminary mentors, like everybody else, talked of spiritual growth in terms of one's relationship with God. But I have come to realize that the essence of spirituality is what happens in us; one's relationship with God might have nothing to do with the matter.

Granted that one dimension of the human mind is spiritual, simply integrating that dimension would transform a person spiritually. Like a NASA space probe zooming into space right on target, increasing personal integration would advance a person along the trajectory of the open-ended expansion toward which the human spirit tends. Such a person would live with a sense of wonder and awe, respectful of our world and its life forms, reverent toward all other beings. On occasion, such a person might also experience moments of union with all that is: he or she would have a mystical experience.

This understanding is wholly humanistic. It is a psychological explanation of spiritual growth. But traditional explanations—like those I heard growing up and like those which most people in the West still accept—appeal ultimately to God and understand spiritual growth as a result of divine grace in the soul or some such thing.

Well, does God fit into my explanation?

At this point, I only insist that God does fit in, and I will eventually explain how. However, *God* will have to mean something different from what most popular piety takes it to mean. Such an outcome should be no surprise. After all, the spiritual quest that I have been describing is a project for adults, and most of us retain only our childhood understanding of God and religion. Growing maturity in spiritual things should naturally bring with it a changed notion of God.

Mixing God up in the matter tends to produce a muddle. The result of the muddle is less personal growth rather than more, and more religious nonsense rather than true spirituality.

It is one thing to speak of God as God really is and quite another to speak of our notions of "God." In the end, I do not pretend to know what God really is. To comprehend God, one would need to be God. Still, I do insist that some notions of God are better than others—not to say fully what God is, but to delineate what God is not and to suggest what God is most likely to be. It only stands to reason that the pursuit of spiritual growth would require one to develop a more refined, more subtle, and more accurate notion of God. In chapter 18 I spell out what I believe to be the best available notion of God. In the meantime, I want to explain why I keep keeping God out of the picture.

Reasons for a Nontheological Approach

I have taken a nontheological approach to spiritual growth for a number of reasons. Most importantly, as I believe I have shown, we can explain almost everything about spirituality without bringing God into the picture. If this assertion is true, it would be better to leave God out—and I believe God would applaud such a move—because mixing God up in the matter tends to produce a muddle. The result of the muddle is less personal growth rather than more, and more religious nonsense rather than true spirituality. My scientist's mind would argue that the proof is in the pudding. And with this book I am offering a new recipe.

Another consideration is that in our day many people have rejected religion. They question or outright deny its teachings about God. Therefore, it is counterproductive to present the spiritual quest in terms of a relationship with God. Many people would not be receptive even though they may well be sincerely seeking spiritual guidance. So, for those who want it, I offer an understanding of spirituality that leaves God out of the picture, but again for those who want it, I offer an understanding that also makes room for God understood in a refined way.

Another reason I take a humanistic approach relates to my personal journey. At this point in my life, my project is that of a psychologist. I come to this topic with the questions of a scientist. Accordingly, my goal is to provide a rigorous and coherent account of spirituality grounded in evidence. Additionally, I teach at a state university. I would be violating professional boundaries by advocating any particular religion in my classes, lectures, or professional conferences. Besides, being a theologian as well as a psychologist, I know the difference between theology and psychology, and I know how the two relate. I do not think it proper, or necessary, to bring God into my psychological work.

I have been surprised that, in the name of openness to spirituality, many of my psychological colleagues insist on inserting God into psychology. Once, at a weeklong course I offered on spirituality for psychological professionals, one woman stormed out of the classroom in protest after the first day. She had enrolled in that course specifically, she said, to learn how to make God a part of her clinical practice. She was unhappy when I asserted that psychologists have no credentials to bring God into treatment unless they are clergy or trained theologians.

More recently, in a 2001 issue of *Counseling and Values*, my ideas on spirituality in *secular* psychotherapy were the topic of discussion. Three full-length articles criticized my position for being irreligious and godless. Evidently, my colleagues were unable to understand spirituality apart from religion or God: even in professional circles, there is much confusion about these matters.

Commonly, commitment to science is breaking down, and argument by appeal to evidence does not hold the respect it once did. People are claiming the right to hold opinions just because they like them, so religious belief is supposed to pass without criticism or analysis. Under these circumstances, though it may be unwelcome, a hard-nosed scientific treatment of spiritual and religious matters is just what is needed.

Presenting spirituality scientifically, understanding it as an aspect of psychology, I feel obliged to find a way to treat the subject apart from theology. My personal quest and my professional obligation have pushed me to discover and refine that way. In the process, I have experimented with my own spiritual life and with my sanity. I have learned some things along the way, and these I want to share here.

Alternatives for a Shrinking World

Finally, I believe that the current state of our world calls for a nontheological approach to spirituality. We live on a shrinking planet, and we are being forced to forge a global community. In the past, individual communities found unity in their particular shared sets of beliefs and ethics; every people had its particular gods, rites, and rituals—its own religion. We are now, all of us, well aware that there are many religions and that in significant ways they all differ.

In this situation, I can imagine a global community emerging in only two ways. Either one society and its religion will dominate the globe and impose its ways on everyone else. I do not see how this solution could be successful. The United States is the most likely candidate for this role of global bully, and already we see violent opposition to U.S. domination. Such violence will continue, and understandably so, unless another solution is found.

The alternative is to come up with a spiritual vision, a set of beliefs and ethics, that every human being could embrace in good conscience. The only vision that could qualify must be grounded in the very workings of the human mind. Such a vision would then be natural, something common to all humanity, yet such a vision could remain open to a variety of expressions, fit an array of different cultures, and be embodied in a range of different religions. Common commitment to a human core of spirituality could unite a global community, and specific variations beyond that core would allow for personal, cultural, and religious differences.

I believe that the understanding of spirituality I am presenting is that human core of spirituality. Or if it is not, such a human core is what I am aiming at, and I welcome the input of kindred spirits to help formulate that core spirituality. Come what may, one thing is clear: that core cannot require belief in God—because people have very different notions of God, some goodwilled people reject God altogether, and there is no way to ever prove opinions about God.

For decades I have been on a quest for spiritual understanding. Now I am proposing an understanding of spirituality for which explicit reference to God is not essential, although this understanding can open onto belief in God. Deeply concerned about the state of our world, I present a humanistic explanation of spiritual growth. I believe that such an explanation is what our world needs today. I say more about this project in the next chapter.

CHAPTER 16

Spirituality and/or Religion

M OST PEOPLE UNDERSTAND spirituality in terms of a relationship with God. But I am proposing to explain what "a relationship with God" means on its human side. Once achieved, this explanation makes appeal to God unnecessary. Talk of God is the scaffolding that got us to this next level. Once there, we can dismantle the scaffolding. For all practical purposes, God then becomes irrelevant, and with God, in some way so does religion.

What I am saying is deeply disturbing—at least it is to me. In various ways, I have dedicated my entire life to religion. I certainly could never have survived thus far without my intensely religious commitment. Yet here I am saying religion is irrelevant, and my religious commitment itself is what makes me say so. As I ponder these matters, I realize that we are at a peculiar moment in history. Whereas religion was what gave many of us inspiration and vision, at this point religion may be more the problem than the solution.

Religion portrays an understanding of life. Religion provides a set of answers to the big questions: Where did we come from? Where are we going? Why are we here? What is worth living for? What's it all about? And religion generally expects people to believe the answers that are given. Religion expects people to be committed. Besides, the answers to such questions don't work for us unless we really believe them.

But there are many religions, and they propose different answers. At some level anyone deeply committed to his or her own religion just has to disagree with members of another religion. Perhaps she or he will openly oppose the others—and religion-based conflict has been the glaring outrage of the last half a century: the atrocities of our age make the Muslim conquests, the Crusades, the Inquisition, and the Reformation's wars of religion look like schoolyard bullying. At least secretly in his or her heart, the deeply religious person will write the others off—and this response has also characterized our era: "religious tolerance" and "loving the sinner but hating the sin" and "charity" toward a person "known" to be "going to hell." Such attitudes are no basis for world unity. At best, deep religious conviction of this sort allows only for mutual tolerance. Such deeply held religious conviction revives the Cold War on a global scale.

Religion and the Religious

The disturbing problem is this: no deeply committed religious persons—including most clergy, lay ministers, and any true believers—can be part of the solution to our global challenge. The more firmly they believe, the bigger a problem they become. In all goodwill, the only way true believers know to help others is to convert them to their religion. But if they do not convert, the believers must see them as infidels, misguided, and at some level dangerous.

The twentieth century's fundamentalisms—Jewish, Christian, and Muslim—provide the obvious example. At some point, a deeply committed religious person must set up barriers between people. Thus, in the name of religion, we see bizarre developments. Religious groups isolate themselves in self-protective enclaves. They not only have their own beliefs, their own religious services, and their own schools, but they also set up their own neighborhoods and community centers, their own clothing styles, their own stores and businesses, their own radio and TV stations—and, worst of all, even their own media campaigns to try and get others to join their xenophobic movement. While the world moves toward a global community, religious groups move toward social division.

Surely, these developments violate religion at its best: love, compassion, care for others, concern for the common good, community. To be true to the spirit of religion today, you can hold to your own religion only lightly. Any absolute grip is bound to be limiting and oppositional. To be religious religiously today is unacceptable; it makes you part of the problem. Today, paradoxically, you have to be a religious believer without really believing wholeheartedly.

Holding firmly to our religion leaves us in a bind, but there is a workable alternative. It does not require that we reject religion outright. It requires that we rethink our religious commitments and expand and realign them. It calls for a daunting spiritual quest.

The solution is to sort out different facets of religion and to realize that some are more essential than others. Then one can hold very firmly to the essentials and very lightly to the rest. This "sorting out" is precisely what I'm doing in this book. I proposed a humanistic spirituality, and it easily fits into religion—but only as long as religion is supremely respectful of it, and in this case it will actually be in control. It will be the essential.

I see spirituality as one facet of religion. In my mind spirituality concerns all those "good things" about religion—love, compassion, concern for the common good, community, personal growth, and the like. These things pertain to us as human beings making our way together positively through life right here on planet Earth. Understood in this way, spirituality is different from other key facets of religion: doctrines, dogmas, beliefs. Too often, these pertain to supposed nonhuman and other-worldly realities.

The doctrines, the metaphysical beliefs, are the crux of the problem. Ironically, they were originally proclaimed in every case, I believe, precisely to foster the good things of this earth. They were to offer an overarching framework for a fulfilling individual and communal life. For example, belief in God and obedience to God were intended to make us live together in peace—even as Jesus taught that love of God and love of neighbor are two sides of the same coin. Or again, to insist that God is a trinity of divine persons implied that we, too, should live as unique individuals but in enduring community. But once proclaimed, doctrines tend to become rigid and opaque. In any movement, second and third generations lose the creativity of the founders. Then, the original wisdom-filled teachings get taken for exotic and esoteric knowledge. They get turned into abstract dogmas, distant formulas. Being enforced, not lived, they project a religious world out of synch with earthly life. And when religious worlds collide, we have problems.

Doctrines differ from religion to religion, so insistence on them undermines human community. Absolute commitment to principles of love, justice, and wholesome living is precisely what we need today. We can do without screeching preaching about other-worldly, doctrinal claims.

Untestable Dogma

I use the Western terms *doctrines* and *dogmas*, but all religions have a metaphysical superstructure of beliefs. Western

Christian doctrines are well known: the existence of God, the inspiration of the Bible, special revelations to chosen spokespersons for God, a trinity of persons in God, the divinity of Jesus, the resurrection of Jesus, the afterlife in heaven, the eternity of family life. Eastern religions have their own beliefs: a multiplicity of gods, the illusionary nature of physical reality, the nonreality of the self, past lives, karma, reincarnation, the cycle of cosmic collapse and reformation. In the modern and postmodern world, doctrines have not gone away. New Age religion also has its doctrines—life as a school, channeled messages, spiritual entities, celestial libraries, angels, realms, energies, crystals, vibrations.

All of us will see something on those lists as sheer fancy. Surely, we chuckle at this or that item of other people's beliefs. But here is the problem: we will not all agree on what is fancy and what is fact, if any of it is factual at all. "One person's meat is another's poison." And there is no way to determine the difference.

Science speaks of claims that cannot be proved one way or the other as "nonfalsifiable." The term implies that the claim has no detectible consequences, so there is no way to show that the claim could be false. No outcome could ever disprove the claim. Said in reverse, if something is true, it will show. If it does not show one way or the other, why believe it is true? Many religious teachings are nonfalsifiable.

It is said that God answers prayers. If you pray and do not get what you want, does this outcome disprove that claim? No. You will be told, perhaps, that you didn't pray properly or that God knows what is best for you and will give you what you really need. Or else, to put it bluntly, that God did answer but the answer was no. The failure of the prayer will never show that belief in prayer is mistaken. The claim about the power of prayer is nonfalsifiable. Take it or leave it and nothing changes.

It makes no practical difference. There is no possible evidence that could make believers abandon the claim.

The existence of God presents a similar case (at this point let's not even get into what "God" means). Granted that the world does exist and continues on its way, what difference would it make to affirm the existence of God or deny it? None whatsoever. The world goes on. Even Jesus said that God lets the rain fall on the just and the unjust.

I delight to remember an incident that happened with a clever friend of mine. Truly a good person, he happens not to be very religious. We were in Boston, and I had some business in Harvard Square. He had a car and offered to drive me there—a heroic prospect, at best. Even worse, we were going to need a parking space—an impossible dream. Well, as we turned into the square, there before us was an empty space, just sitting there, no rush of cars toward it, no drivers cursing one another to reach it, no pedestrian blocking it until a cohort could bring the car around. We pulled right in. Right in Harvard Square. My friend commented wryly, "See how God takes care of those who don't believe in Him."

And to the extent that beliefs cannot be proved or disproved, they can be considered irrelevant to an understanding of spiritual development.

Talk of God projects another realm, out of this world. That supposed realm is beyond any adjudication. People can make it out to be whatever they want, and nobody can prove them wrong, and they cannot prove themselves right. Believe in God or not, you might still find a parking space.

If we are honest about it, many religious beliefs seem to be mere opinion. They project a world that may or may not be true, but there is no way of knowing. Did God on Mount Sinai really give Moses the Ten Commandments on stone tablets? Is God really Father, Son, and Holy Ghost? Is Allah (God) really only One and Muhammad, his final prophet? Is God male, or is the Goddess actually the source that enlivens all things? Did the Angel Moroni really bring Joseph Smith revelations written in Reformed Egyptian on now-lost gold plates? After death will we really return in another form to relive this life again and again until we get it right? All of these beliefs are nonfalsifiable. Nothing could show they are false, but does this fact mean they are, therefore, true? This much is sure: they cannot all be true.

What Beliefs Offer

Such beliefs make up the metaphysical superstructure of religions. These beliefs are the part of religion that people need to hold only lightly. To be sure, some of these beliefs are more reasonable than others. Some can be shown to be plausible or, at least, not impossible. Some support wholesome living. Nonetheless, there is no way to prove or disprove any of them. And to the extent that beliefs cannot be proved or disproved, they can be considered irrelevant to an understanding of spiritual development.

Oh, they may be personally significant. They may afford consolation in troubled times. They may foster kindness and concern. They may provide motivation. They may help make things make sense. And to this extent, they may be useful. They may, indeed, have practical implications.

But the usefulness always comes back to this world: consolation, kindness, motivation, good sense. We know nothing certain of a life after death or a life before life. We rely on usefulness in this world to judge these beliefs, and we rely on investigation of life in this world—well-done scientific research—to tell us what is really useful. No longer relying on supposed revelation or the traditions of the elders, we have learned how to discover for ourselves what actually fosters life or destroys it. Thus, religious beliefs about some other world have become dispensable. And where they are thought to be indispensable, they are a problem.

We humans are a peculiar lot: "none so queer as folk." We created religious worlds so that we could survive in spite of this life's uncertainties; yet global survival is now forcing us to dismantle our religious worlds. I feel bad to be writing such things. I wonder if I am not pulling the rug out from under people. I fear I am destroying the religious faith that gets most of us through life.

Yet I do not think it is I who am doing this terrible deed. World events and personal growth have brought us to this point. There is no avoiding the challenge. People are already raising the questions that I address here. You would not be reading this book, I suspect, if you were not already doubting your religion or, at least, looking for something more. Religious uncertainty is pandemic these days. To push the process to its natural conclusion may not be a bad thing.

A Deeper Faith

Besides, these thoughts do not actually call us to give up our faith. Rather, they call us to deeper and purer faith. If faith means trust rather than blind assent to doctrines, more than ever we need faith. Only increased trust will take us to the next level.

My lifelong spiritual quest has brought me to a faith free from dogma: trust. My presentation also invites you to such faith. After all, the deep lesson of meditative practice is to let go of all thoughts, feelings, and images and to let things be. During meditative practice, even thoughts about God are to be dismissed as driftings of the mind. The rules of meditation also apply to life. The very goal of long-term meditation is to integrate its experience into everyday living. The lesson is to let go of the ideas that structure and distort our living. The lesson is to live in the ever-new here-and-now, refreshingly open to what actually is.

To let things be is to live in faith. To let things be is to live with trust and openness. In the face of the unknown, we need openness and trust. They are our only hope for engaging the future buoyantly. Confronting the inevitable uncertainties of life, we need to experience what's there, to marvel at it and ponder it, and to expand ourselves and our world to include an ever-unfolding reality. We can only do so if we are open and trusting. Unless our wisdom is the open-ended wisdom that I am presenting, pretending that we already know the truth—and even worse, insisting that others agree—is not a truly religious way to live. Pretending that we know is not trusting in God; rather, it is self-serving dogmatism. It shuts life down and boxes us in and eventually leads to a dead end. It is not faith; it is totalitarianism.

My hope is that this humanistic understanding of spirituality will ultimately be freeing—liberating for each of us individually and liberating for the whole human race. Freed from unbudging commitment to metaphysical speculation, we can be more committed to life in this world, and we can be more open to realizing all that this life holds. Committed to wholesome living on this planet, we need not fear eternal damnation. On the contrary, living this life well, we are all the more likely to qualify also for whatever life-to-come there might be. The next chapter will remind us how big our lives in this world—our spiritual lives—actually are.

CHAPTER 17

Confusing the Spiritual and the Divine

ADULTS SOMETIMES MAKE FUN OF "puppy love." Such jest is really unfair. Yes, naïve infatuation is a far cry from true and profound love. But infatuation must also be a stepping-stone to true love, and in many ways the innocence and beauty of puppy love point to the genuine thing. So puppy love needs to be treasured. Nonetheless, it is not the genuine thing. Only long experience, the pain of heartbreak, and hard-won maturity bring a person to the point of understanding genuine love and, perhaps, actually achieving it. In the meantime, often adults pursue love affairs more laughable than puppy love. For years, perhaps a lifetime, we can live under illusions and confuse imitations with the real thing. We do the same regarding spiritual matters. We take moving experiences of our own spiritual capacity to be literally experiences of God.

The human spirit is an open-ended dynamism. It leads us to ever broader experience, ever deeper understanding, ever wider reality, and ever more profound love. In the ideal, the reach of the human spirit is unbounded. It is open to all there is to be known and loved. Experience of your own spiritual capacity in a moment of deep meditation might leave you believing you had experienced the infinite. When so wondrous an experience occurs, no wonder people talk of experiencing God. But is this experience necessarily an experience of God? Or is it "only" an experience of your own human spirit?

Our spiritual capacity reaches out to bring things together. The ultimate goal of the spirit is that all would be one. You can see this tendency of the human spirit in any learning experience—driving a car, mastering a new computer program, taking an algebra course. Once you "get it," the thing is simple. You just do it. If someone asks you how, you say, "Oh, just like this." You forget how long it took to learn each step along the way. Now it all seems like one operation. All the facets have come together. In one composite understanding, you know the whole thing through and through. Watch a child learning to tie a shoe, and you'll remember how complicated seemingly simple things can be. Reread a book that was originally a challenge, and you'll be surprised how simple it now is. Once mastered by the human mind, everything is simple. One idea includes the whole lot. The human mind moves toward unity. The human spirit brings all things together as one.

Projecting a Religious World

That unifying function of the spirit operates on every little facet of life. But it also operates on life as a whole. When the big questions arise—What's it all about?—the human mind again wants an answer that makes sense of everything. So when our answers run out—for example, in the face of death, loss, loneliness, illness, or unspeakable tragedy—our minds go forward, nonetheless, and we project an answer big enough to cover all the bases. We project a worldview that goes beyond the here and now. We affirm a God who is in control of the whole universe. We speak of a God whose ways surpass our ways, whose reasons go beyond our ken. In this way, we propose an explanation that makes sense of everything. We make all things hang together. In the process, we create religion, and it includes a world beyond this present one, a world governed by God and populated with powers and spirits. Then, even if we do not understand, we can believe that things do make sense. Our own minds compel us to do so, and to trust our minds is, indeed, a good thing.

Meditative experience can actually confirm our projected religious world. In a transcendent meditative moment we do pass from our current everyday world and into another world. In fact, if we are alert and alive, even during our ordinary waking hours, we are making a new world for ourselves bit by bit every day. But in deep meditation, the powerful transcendent quality of that moment of transition can hook us, so to speak. We want to get hold of that moment and keep it permanently—hence, the rule of meditation to let go of any thought or feeling, no matter how profound it may seem. But we get hooked, nonetheless. And we project that oh-so-normal moment of self-transcendence into another world. We imagine a "spiritual realm," some supposed parallel universe. We talk of a spiritual world, in contrast to this physical world—as if the human world in which we actually live were not itself also, in part, spiritual and as if that spiritual dimension of our actual world were not what we had actually experienced in that moment of heightened awareness.

We talk of a spiritual world, and it promises the comfort and reassurance we want. So we look to that world as an escape from the pain of our human condition. We begin to seek those transcendent moments and start to force our meditative practice. We begin to believe that achieving altered states of consciousness is what meditation and the spiritual quest are about. We end up right back where this book and I began, believing that spiritual fulfillment means having raptures, seeing visions, hearing voices, achieving out-of-body experiences. So we develop a "spiritual life" to give ourselves an inside track on life and to supposedly let us avoid all of life's messiness. We think we deserve this exemption from the challenge of living because we are "spiritual," "enlightened," "holy": good little girls and boys and—I remember myself here—we think we deserve special treatment. Instead of using meditation to lead more wondrous lives right here in our everyday world, we use meditation to try and live in some other world. In the name of spirituality, we construct a fantasy world. And many will support us in this project: much religion is a movement of sustained mass delusion.

In some cases the search for another world gives way to absolutes, and enthusiasts affirm that other world with a vengeance. Supposedly, it is the really real. And this everyday world in which we live is downgraded to a learning experience, a shadow copy, a gross emanation, or an illusion. Reality gets split into two, the physical and the spiritual. In full-blown dualism the physical may even be deemed evil, and only the spiritual is considered worthwhile.

Dualism in Western Tradition

The process that I am describing in general terms is the actual story of Plato and the later development of Plato's thought called Neoplatonism. The spiritual experience of intellectual insight absolutely wowed Plato. He was struck by Pythagoras's theorem about the right triangle: $a^2 + b^2 = c^2$. This formula applies to any right triangle, everywhere and always, and the triangle the theorem envisages is absolutely perfect. No one could actually draw a triangle in this world that would fit the formula precisely; if nothing else, the thickness of the lines would make the drawn triangle imperfect in contrast to the abstract formula. In fact, nothing we can engineer in this world is absolutely perfect. Where can we find a perfect circle? A perfectly square corner? A perfectly level floor? Plato concluded that ideas are the unchanging, eternal, true reality and that the things of this world are only imperfect imitations. He proposed that there is actually a World of Ideas where these perfect and changeless "realities" exist. Following suit, he and his followers suggested that the human being is a spirit imprisoned in a body, and that the goal of life is to free oneself from the imperfections of the physical world and to achieve a purely spiritual existence.

The fact that we have a spiritual capacity within us
does not mean that we are God.

That thinking flowed into Christianity in its early centuries. The result was the now standard beliefs that we are body and soul, that the soul separates from the body at death, that the soul is immortal, and that it will live forever in heaven, its true home. Other Christian beliefs never were fully reconciled with Platonic thought: the incarnation—en*flesh*ment!—of God in Christ, the presence of Christ in his *earthly* followers, and the resurrection of the *body*. For the sake of comforting belief in a spiritual world, we just overlook the inconsistencies. The alternative approach, which I am suggesting here, also has its price: living with ambiguity and uncertainty.

Thinking similar to Platonism flows through Western Gnosticism, most Eastern philosophy and religion, and many strands of today's New Religion. The upshot of it all is the downgrading of our everyday world as mere passing appearance and the exaltation of a purely spiritual world as the really real. We imagine that our real life is in some other world.

Identifying the Spiritual and the Divine

One further step was taken in the development of Western religion. Not only did early Christian thinkers use Neoplatonic thought to forge new beliefs about us human beings, our world, and our ultimate end, they also tried to integrate Neoplatonic philosophy with Christian belief in the Creator-God. They turned Plato's supposed World of Ideas, where all things exist in perfection, into the mind of God, and the ideas themselves became God's eternal thoughts, the "blueprints" according to which God created the world. The World of Ideas, the spiritual world, became heaven, the realm of God. In effect, those thinkers identified the spiritual with the divine. They took the marvel of "ordinary" human insight and turned it into a divine happening. They viewed the human intellect as God's own mind inside us. They projected "merely" human capacities into a sharing in divinity. They suggested that, because we are spiritual, deep down inside we are really God.

I have described how the mingling of Greek and Christian thought ended up identifying the spiritual with the divine. Whether or not this identification is correct is another question. And, of course, people are free to believe what they want. Indeed, as I argued in chapter 15, in matters of God and the afterlife, there is no way to prove an opinion correct or false anyway. Nonetheless, understanding how the spiritual got to be identified with the divine might help to support my insistence: this identification is a mistake. Two very different realities—the empirically verifiable human spirit and a metaphysically asserted God—were mixed together.

From there it was only one short step to the suggestion that our minds are really a part of the mind of God or even that we ourselves are really God: our innermost being is a "spark of divinity." This suggestion should not sound novel to anyone. It is common enough throughout history and common in contemporary thinking. Of course, I think it is mistaken. The mistake is precisely to confuse the spiritual with the divine. The fact that we have a spiritual capacity within us does not mean that we are God. This capacity might make us godlike, somehow similar to God—because we can conceive ideas that are unchanging, timeless, or perfect and because in largeness of spirit we can love and affirm whatever there is of good anywhere, in some way transcending space and time—but this capacity does not make us God.

Likewise, it is jumping to conclusions to say that we experience God when, in profound meditation or on some other occasion, we know a moment of self-transcendence. As I have suggested, the human spiritual capacity already explains those transcendent experiences. There is a straightforward enough explanation of mysticism. Highly publicized, recent research on religious experience and the brain is even suggesting what parts of the brain are involved in those experiences and how the brain could produce such experiences. Unfortunately, some neuroscientists are pandering to a popular audience and talking in terms of the ludicrous notion of "God in the brain." There is no need to implicate God in the matter. In transcendent moments we experience our own selves, and we are very large, indeed. The self-transcending openness of our human spirits is unlimited in scope. So meditation and transcendent experience are not about the experience of God, nor are they about moving into some supposed, other-worldly, spiritual realm. Meditation is "merely" an exercise of being ever more fully present to the here and now and experiencing in this full presence the wonder of ourselves and our world.

A Life without Easy Certainties

But where does such a hard-nosed understanding leave us? If we just have ourselves here and now, isn't our situation rather dismal?

Sometimes we do feel the weight of the world on our poor, burdened shoulders. The superficiality and mechanization of contemporary culture often leave us feeling isolated and lonely.

Besides, to some extent, the sense that "it's all up to me" is accurate. Our life is our own and no one else's. There are things in life that no one can do in our stead. In some unavoidable ways, we have to face and live our lives alone. On the other hand, we do have our gifts, our talents, and our opportunities, and we do have one another. Together in goodwill, we can make this life a beautiful thing. And open to the depths of life through purified minds, we can delight in the daily minor "miracles" of our existence. Our lives are well worth living.

But when my life is over, when I die, is that the absolute end? Do I and all my world with me simply cease to exist?

Perhaps.

Maybe.

There is no way to answer this question with certainty. The uncomfortableness of this indefinite answer is what leads us and religion to project another world, a world of pure spirit and eternity, a world of assurance and guaranteed fulfillment. If we wish, we can bank on that world. We can invest our hopes in an afterlife. We can live for another world. Easily enough we will certainly find fellow believers to shore up our doubts.

Or else we could embrace the uncertainty of our fate and choose to live open-eyed with it. We could own that we live with mystery, surrounded by unknowing. Far from making us calloused or unprincipled, this burning awareness could make us humble and loving. We could expend ourselves in this world, making the most of the time we have. We could pour out our best for the sake of all that is right, wholesome, and good. We could put trust in life, which is bigger than we are, not fearing to use ourselves up in the process of dedicated living. At the same time, we could still continue to hope—but no more than hope—that the marvelous beauty of human life does, indeed, somehow partake of eternity and that somehow we, with our loved ones and all humankind, will ever be part of it.

On occasions when very hard pressed, we might use meditation to confront the uncertainty with which we live. In meditative moments of induced quiet and deep inner calm, we might face the unknown naked and eyeball-to-eyeball, and in that respectful standoff the unknown would lose its frightening force. Such is the effect of consistent meditative practice. I can attest so from my own experience. At times when, deeply discouraged and thinking that all life is a sham, I sat myself down in determined meditation and like a stubborn S.O.B. stared down the black uncertainty of it all, refusing to back off, facing off with God Almighty himself—if this is what I was doing—and I emerged alive from this bold endeavor, not struck down by lightning or condemned to hell, but strengthened and re-affirmed in the very core of my being.

Despite the unknowing, uncertainty, and mystery that inevitably surround our living, by honestly facing our demons we can walk on with dignity; we can live with honor and a gentle pride that only comes with reverence and humility. Then we might truly know the mystical path, and we would identify with the spiritual giants of all the world's religions who knew not just ecstasy, rapture, and bliss, but also nothingness, emptiness, and the void. I have been surprised on numerous occasions, going to meditation feeling disheartened, only to rise with renewed energy, overflowing purpose, and deeply felt confidence. The tapped power of the human spirit can transform our perspective. Calmly and resolutely facing the ultimate threats to life frees us from their power: we are no longer on the run from their menacing pursuit.

Fortified with daily spiritual exercise, our lives are richer, and we are a blessing to all we meet. We are filled with gratitude and walk on with awe. We readily acknowledge the Great Mystery before which we exist. We are moved from the heart to bow in honest respect to the Unknown from which we come and to which we know that we go. We no longer confuse a "mere" experience of the spiritual with an experience of God. Yet, in our own way—a more valid way, I believe—we again stand before God. As when grown beyond infatuation and experiencing genuine love, we discover the true God of the Universe.

The next chapter pursues this line of thinking.

CHAPTER 18

God and Spiritual Experience

"Toyland, Toyland, beautiful girl and boy land." So runs the popular song. There is also the song: "Jesus loves the little children, all the children of the world." Both songs come out of the same mold: they speak to the fantasy and wonder that is such a beautiful part of childhood. Like everything else, our religion is rooted in the early world of childish make-believe. Unlike most other things, however, our religion often never branches beyond that world. We grow up physically, emotionally, and intellectually, but do we mature religiously?

We learn about God as children, and what we learn as children takes root. That lesson gets lodged deep in our psyches. So most of us have a child's notion of God, and we hold onto it. To this extent Freud was right: for most of us "God" is Daddy (and Mommy) writ large in the sky.

If we were lucky as children, someone was always there when we needed help. When we were tottering and ready to fall, somehow a hand miraculously caught us. When we scraped our knee, on the spot someone appeared to wipe away our tears. When we needed money for an ice cream with friends, a parent made sure empty pockets did not embarrass us. And we just took for granted that such care would always be there. Somehow, almost magically, we assumed our needs would be met. As we grow up, the dawning realization that Christmas doesn't just happen, that someone must make it happen, is often disturbing. We pine for Christmases past. We want to remain children.

That needs get met was also the lesson of religion. The Great Need-Meeter was God. As someone phrased the matter, God is the adult version of Santa Claus. When we finally see through the fairy tale of Santa Claus, we can still have God, and many of us—most, if the truth be told—use God in that very way.

Petitionary Prayer

To this day I catch myself in times of trouble praying to God for magical help. Despite all my education and life experience, I find my early learning responding in me like a reflex: "God, please make my car start this time" or "God, don't let me be getting sick" or "God, let there be more money in my checking account than I think there is." So I stop myself, correct my thought, and forbid myself from turning God into my Personal Problem Solver. I remind myself of the Great Unknown, ever present and ever acting. Then I turn to my problem as an adult, taking responsibility for it myself, seeking help from others as needed, backing off for a rest if I must. Like the other driftings of my mind at which I catch myself in meditation practice, I use my reflex-like calls to a child's Santa Claus God to remind myself to come back to reality where, if anywhere, God can be found. I carry the practice of meditation over into my daily life. I temper my childish longings for the distant God of fantasy, and I practice living instead with the Mysterious Presence in the here and now.

I don't believe I'm alone in my habit of calling on God in a childish way. The most common form of prayer is petition: we ask God for things. Even the most sophisticated of believers, I have found, secretly harbors a hope of miraculous interventions.

We want to believe that "God" will suspend the very laws of the universe to make things turn out our way. Phrased so bluntly, this belief seems obviously misguided. Yet simplistic religion eggs us on: "Nothing is impossible to God," "Miracles do happen," "More is wrought by prayer than the world imagines."

Of course, prayer of petition can be understood in a positive way. Each of those sayings can be given a valid meaning. Prayer of petition is not necessarily a psychologically unwholesome behavior. Most obviously, such prayer can be taken to express an honest and humble acknowledgement: we are not fully in control of our lives; even in the most mundane of affairs—the healing of an ingrown toenail!—we live in trust and hope. Taken in a nuanced sense, prayer of petition can express the same attitude as meditation: letting go. To pray to God for something can mean to surrender control over it: "Let go, and let God." Yet this nuanced sense is hard to come by, and attempts to express it provoke defensive reactions. The fact remains that a most common notion of God is the Great Miracle Worker in the Sky—the Cosmic Santa Claus.

God as Creator

A more adequate notion of God is Creator—that which set things in being, sustains them in being, and allows them to function according to their particular natures. The medievals called these three aspects of God's creative work creation, conservation, and concurrence. This notion of Creator is the most plausible understanding I know for the Great Mystery. The fact of existence—not what things are or how they operate, but that they are—is the key to the mystery of God. As philosophers have posed the question, "Why is there something, rather than nothing?" Why is it that things exist and go on existing? Why does anything exist at all? It is with the fact of existence, with

the mere fact of being, that one comes face to face in meditation. When all thoughts, feelings, and images are swept aside,
what remains is "mere" existence. Things are. They continue to
be. In the stillness of quiet moments, they remain there. They
do nothing. Nothing is afoot. Things just are.

I remember a cartoon of two Buddhist monks sitting in
meditation, one an elder, the other obviously a novice. The
elder was responding to a question the other had asked: "Nothing happens next. This is it."

That response reminds me of my own experiences in an
empty church. A lone candle may flicker; a breeze might whis-
per against a windowpane. Otherwise, nothing. The altar, flow-
ers, statues, pillars, paintings on the walls—things just stand
there. Nothing happens. I pray my childish prayer to God—and
nothing. No answer, no nonanswer, no indication whatsoever
that my prayer made any difference. Everything is just there in
stillness. In my own stillness I might realize that, like all those
other things, I, too, am just there. Oh, unlike those inanimate
objects I am aware of my being there—but I am just there, we
are all just here. That we are aware of our existence does not
mean that we are the source of it. Just like every other thing in
the universe, we just happen to be. We could, as well, not happen to be. There is no necessity in our existence. We come, and
we go. So does everything else. The fact of existence is a mystery.

What is existence? What is this "being there"? What is the
experience of just being? It is the light side of the Great Mystery.
It is all that shows of the Dark Void and the Great Unknown—
that things *are*.

Whatever it is that accounts for the fact that things are is
"God." "God" is a name we put on that Great Unknown. Legitimately we ask how is it that there is something rather than
nothing. And legitimately we expect a coherent answer. But the
only answer we come up with is "God"—which is not really an

answer at all, but only the name we put on the expected answer that we seek. In solving an algebraic equation, we let *X* name the unknown. Similarly, in pondering the existence of things, we let *God* stand for the Great Unknown.

God as the Unknown

"God" names the expected answer to a legitimate question. If we are to trust the inborn orientation of our own minds, legitimate questions do have answers, so the question about existence must have an answer. Not knowing that answer, we call it "God." Thus, to believe in God is not an irrational thing. On the contrary, to believe in God is to trust our own minds. To believe in God is to believe in ourselves.

That believing in God is actually believing in ourselves does not mean that God is just an idea we make up. The point is not that God is merely a favorite fantasy in which we want to believe. Rather, the point is that we can come up with ideas that are actually correct. On the basis of trust in the workings of our own minds, our idea about God can be as valid as our ideas about anything else. After all, in whatever we claim to know, we are just trusting our own most careful and most honest understanding; we are going with our collective best shot. And we can do no other.

Still, having the name "God" as an answer to our question about the existence of things should not make us think that we know anything more than we did when we asked the question and expected that it had an answer. We do not understand the answer that we give. We just have a code name for the answer, whatever It might be: G-O-D. Other religions give It other names. The *Star Wars* series calls It "the Force." Whatever the name, beneath all the names lies the same mystery, still unknown.

I do think it legitimate to acknowledge It, that Great Unknown. It must be something. It deserves acknowledgment. The fact that It is behind all things also suggests that It is intelligent and deliberate in Its doings, so it would also be appropriate to speak of It in some way as a Someone. I also think it legitimate to reverence Him/Her/It and to be in awe before Him/Her/It. To do so is simply to be honest about the matter, to be humble before the facts—there surely is something greater than ourselves behind the universe.

Some consider me godless or atheistic because of this theology that I hold. Nonetheless, it seems to me that reverence and awe before the power behind the universe is what "belief in

---

That believing in God is actually believing in ourselves does not mean that God is just an idea we make up. Our idea about God can be as valid as our ideas about anything else.

God" means—not magic, not expectations, not bargains or agreements, not privileged knowledge or special treatment, just reverence or, to use the religious word, worship. This must be the most legitimate of all religious attitudes. The wise grandmother of a Brazilian friend of mine expressed this same idea otherwise: "God is for thanking, not for asking." The most legitimate religious attitude is to appreciate the wonder of existence and to be humble before it. If such an attitude is godless, then I plead guilty.

In my mind, the existence of God is more plausible than our personal existence after death. People often make these two notions into one: just because there is a God, we ourselves must live forever. Supposedly, belief in God also means belief in an afterlife. Interestingly, Judaism does not generally make that connection. Neither am I so sure of it.

After all, it is quite reasonable to expect that there is a force that accounts for the existence of things. But there is really no firm reason that our lives must go on once our physical organisms cease to function. The idea of life after death is problematic if I recognize that I am not a spirit temporarily encased in a body, but a composite of body, psyche, and spirit. If I am, in part, bodily and after death my body goes into the grave, where do I go after I die? I know no existence apart from my body. Even my spiritual experiences, which transcend space and time, depend on the functioning of my organic brain. Yet, on the other hand, transcending space and time through the functioning of my brain, I am also somehow beyond the bodily; I am, in part, also spiritual. Should I not, then, be immune to the effects of physical dissolution? Body, on the one hand, and spirit, on the other: the considerations go back and forth—even as we humans are stretched between heaven and earth. As one philosopher colorfully stated the matter, "We are angels that s--t." In the words of the ruler of Siam in *King and I*, "'Tis a puzzlement." We are a puzzlement to ourselves. And there is no way to resolve this puzzle definitively. Belief in God runs into fewer philosophical problems.

I argued in chapter 17 that we jump to unwarranted conclusions to think that we experience God when we have a transcendent experience. Nonetheless, it is legitimate to say that God is acting in our meditative practice. If the name "God" refers to whatever is ultimately behind the existence and functioning of the universe, then God is acting in and through whatever is. Then God is acting in and through our humanity, including our brains, psyches, and human spirits. To this extent we can rightly say that God is involved in our spiritual growth—because God is involved in everything; nothing would be or function without "God." Obviously, however, this statement does not grant very much. This statement does not make us special in comparison to everything else that also exists. Sorry. I continue to minimize involvement of God in spiritual matters.

God and Meditation

Still, when meditation is the topic, more can be said about God's involvement. Our being as human really is peculiar compared to the being of other things. All things are, but we are also aware that we are. Our being comes under our own scrutiny and, to some extent, then, under our own control. We have something to say about what we will be and become. Moreover, our becoming can move in two directions: it can be positive or negative. We can build up, or we can tear down.

Insofar as the direction of our becoming is positive, insofar as it leads to further being rather than less, we could say that we are moving godward. If most fundamentally "God" is about being, anything that enhances being is godlike. From this point of view, there is another legitimate way in which we can conceive of God. We can see God, not only as Creator, but also as the Fullness of all that is positive, right, and good, of all that has a future, of all that is moving open-endedly onward. From this point of view, a believer could say that meditation enables one to relate ever more perfectly to God.

A believer could say that, and, as I just explained it, to say that would be correct. However, this fact does not mean that the believer who talks of God as well as of meditation is in any better situation than the nonbeliever who just meditates without concern for God. The sum and substance of the experience of both is the same. The transformative effects of the meditation in both cases are the same. The difference is only that the theist—one who believes in God—interprets the meditative experience differently. The theist puts a wider frame on the experience and sees in the picture not only human integration and spiritual growth but also relationship with God.

I would not venture to say that the one who speaks also of God stands in a better place than the one who does not speak of God. If both are honest in their meditative practice and their living, both know fully well that they are dealing with mystery. On the one hand, the theist names God but knows that she or he really does not understand that which is named, so she or he holds only lightly to talk of God. On the other hand, the non-theist is also fully aware of the mystery of existence before which she or he stands and in all honesty and humility would hardly declare definitively that there is no God. Both hold lightly to their metaphysical claims even as both stand in awe before the mystery of existence. As lived, the positions of the honest theist and honest nontheist are hardly far apart. They both seem to be approaching the same point but from opposite directions. In practice, a humble theism comes down in the same place as a humble agnosticism. I would not want to pass judgment on the one or the other.

Of course, what I write here presumes the notion of God that I have developed above. But people can and do believe other-wise. For them God is a Miracle Worker who heeds the pleas of people who obey "His" commands, a Power that guides the comings and goings of life according to divine prerogative, an omnipotent Father or Mother who will intervene to change the flow of things for the benefit of a favorite child. If this is the kind of God in which someone believes, then there is no recon-ciliation between the nonbeliever and the believer. Indeed, on the basis of this believer's childish faith, even the theist I described above must be said not to believe in God at all. Hence, I am called a godless atheist.

One's notion of God is pivotal to this whole discussion. Since we do not really know what God is, people can make God out to be whatever they want, and nobody can prove them wrong. Even on topics that can be proved, people insist on their own beliefs: slavery was actually a benign institution, the Holocaust never happened, and Neil Armstrong never really walked on the moon. I would not waste my time debating about God. People believe what they want to believe. We can only hope that their beliefs don't cause trouble for them—and the rest of us! Argument over metaphysical claims is counterproductive. Arguing merely distracts from the weightier task of responsible living in this world.

I always come back to responsible living in this world, don't I? Nonetheless, my down-to-earth spirituality actually does open onto belief in God, but God understood in a particular way. If all things are to hold together in one coherent whole—as the human mind would want and as traditional religion would insist—then our understanding of God must interlock with our understanding of the universe. Not any notion of God will do. When the spiritual is distinguished from the divine, talk of experiencing God requires nuance. The very structures of our spiritual capacity impose requirements even on our thinking about God. To be an awake, honest, and responsible person in all our dealings requires that we be so also in our religious beliefs. Movement along the spiritual path attunes us to the subtle dimensions of life. That movement also brings with it a refined notion of God. A Santa Claus God just does not fit into this picture.

Obviously, the particular notion of God I propose corresponds to a particular kind of human being. If every notion of God is not as valid as every other, neither is every person as good as every other. What kind of person we are, how we guide our own becoming, does relate to what we might think of God. In many ways, our belief about God is a statement about our beliefs about life. So the issue of proper living—ethics and human authenticity—is the topic of the next chapter.

CHAPTER 19

The Ethical Requirements of Personal Growth

C OMPUTERS CAN BE TERRIFYING. Actually hit that "Enter" key when what you did was wrong, and you cause a disaster. You can lose all your work, erase the program, or get caught in a loop. Computers are great; they can work miracles. But you have to know how to use them—and they seem to have a mind of their own. Being sincere or expressing goodwill just does not cut it. Computers are unforgiving. Make a mistake and you pay for it. To tap the full potential of a computer, you need to use it the way it was programmed. It follows a fixed routine. Violate it, and you only lose. Use it right, and the miracles are yours.

Not God or our belief in God, but our own spiritual nature is the key to our personal growth.

The human spirit is also like that.

The spirit points us to a path of potentially infinite expansion. Our spiritual capacity is open to all there is to be known and loved. Since all things exist through God the Creator, it is even said that God is the ultimate goal of the spiritual quest. Ever more deeply appreciating God's handiwork, we grow ever "nearer" to God. So a theist might say that meditation is part of a godward movement. However conceived, the ideal goal of the human spirit is boundless.

But we humans are peculiar beings. The very spirit that opens us to the universe also makes us free. Because we are aware of things and also aware of our awareness, we stand at a distance from our own experience, so it does not control us. To that extent, we are free agents—and we can use our freedom to undo ourselves. We can make choices that eventually limit our very capacity to choose. Enslavement to drugs is one sad example. Blindness to the truth because of a habit of lying is another. Phrased religiously, such self-undoing "distances" us from God—which is to say, it limits our spiritual capacity and detours our growth from its ideal fulfillment. Like a computer caught in a loop, we block our own effective functioning.

Not God or our belief in God, but our own spiritual nature is the key to our personal growth. So it matters how we use our spiritual capacity. Simply being spiritual does not automatically open us to unlimited unfolding. As I am using the term, being "spiritual" is just a fact of our constitution. We are all spiritual. That is how we are made. We all have a human spirit. Being spiritual is not the same things as growing spiritually. To grow spiritually, we have to use our spiritual capacity well. We have to freely choose to function in accord with the open-ended inclination of the human spirit. Otherwise, we shut our spirits down. Like a herd of buffalo driven to run headlong over a cliff, never to run again, we can use our spiritual capacity to short-circuit that very capacity.

Like everything in the created universe, the human spirit is made in its own peculiar way, and it "works" according to the way it is made. Its very makeup includes requirements for effective functioning. The human spirit has built-in laws of operation.

Personal growth depends on adherence to these laws—not because somebody said so, but because these laws express the very nature of our being. These requirements are built-in. These built-in laws are the essence of ethics or morality.

Being Open-minded

There are four such laws. First, insofar as the human spirit is an unbounded openness, we need to be open-minded. A narrow, close-minded approach to things limits our experiences and shuts out new input. Obviously, we cannot grow and change when we limit our perspectives. As the popular saying has it, "The mind is like a parachute: it works best when it's open."

Of course, it is easy enough to say that we ought to be open. Even if we're deluding ourselves, most of us believe that we already are open-minded. We need this belief to maintain our own sanity. Yet we have all made mistakes, and, if wise, we have learned from them. We know we are incapable of seeing our own blind spots, and surely we are all blind in one way or another. Our blindness is one reason that we need one another. The spiritual quest is not only a personal but also a communal undertaking. Psychologists have even listed ways in which we protect ourselves from unwanted awareness—the defense mechanisms, such as denial, projection, rationalization, displacement, and reaction formation. These operate unconsciously, so our close-mindedness is not always a matter of simple choice. We are victims of our own unaware self-making, and we are products of the physical and social forces that shaped us. Easy to say, being open is not always easy to do. And the same goes for the other core requirements of the spirit that I list below.

We grow in openness when we dedicate ourselves to the project. The requirement to be open poses an ongoing challenge. Increased openness alerts us to the need for even more openness. Openness is a snowballing process. The more we have, the more we get. Many things contribute to openness: thought, study, work, art, travel, relationships, psychotherapy. Meditation is a concentrated form of the quest for openness. Precisely because openness is an essential requirement of the spirit, meditation is a powerful tool for the spiritual quest.

Questioning

Second, insofar as the human spirit seeks understanding and engenders insight, another requirement of the spirit is that we be questioning. All of us have intelligence to one degree or another. We see things, we wonder about them, we want to understand. Healthy spiritual functioning requires indulging this curiosity— and trusting our own minds. For example, when we ask a question and someone gives an answer, we know if our question was answered or not. We may wisely let the thing pass, but we know when we're being "snowed." And when an answer fits, when everything clicks, our very being resonates. If an answer does not make sense, that does not always mean that we cannot understand. Perhaps the proposed answer itself just does not make sense, and for this reason our mind is not satisfied. Being questioning means trusting our capacity to understand.

I remember as a child asking where babies come from. I don't remember what I was told. What I do remember is the distinct impression that the answer I got was silly. It did not credibly address my question. Because of that answer, I also realized that there was something peculiar about this baby thing: adults did not want to talk about it. Completely forgetting the answer I was given, I tucked away in the back of my mind this other lesson. Luckily, I was able to trust my own mind. As a result, I learned something despite the adults who did not want to teach me.

To be questioning means to trust one's own intelligence,

however deep or shallow it might be. The only difference between the highly and slightly intelligent is the time and effort it takes to understand. Unfortunately, many of us give up early. We stop wondering, questioning, asking. We just take things "on faith." We just "shut up and get with the program." We shut down our spiritual functioning.

Being Honest

Third, insofar as the human spirit is aware of its own functioning and questions its own understanding and wants to be sure of its judgments, another spiritual requirement is that we be honest. As Lonergan used to say, "Insights are a dime a dozen." The trick is to have a correct insight. The challenge is to achieve accurate understanding. With an eye to the complete coherence of things, our minds know the difference. So our spirit prompts us to check out our ideas, to compare them to the evidence, to judge their adequacy. The reward of such diligence is that we actually come to know the truth. We go beyond what appears to be the case or what we ourselves might think or want or expect, and we come to know what actually is the case. We gain some real knowledge; we approach closer to reality; we achieve an inkling of truth.

Of course, the prerequisite for knowing the truth is to be honest. Unless we are willing to assess our understandings, to give up our pet theories, to admit our mistakes, and to repeatedly readjust our thinking, we will continue to live in a fantasy world. And we will suffer the consequences when we inevitably trip over reality. Recognizing our illusions is a challenge of spirituality. Moving from fantasy to reality is a feature of the spiritual quest. One of the effects of meditative practice is to make us more present to here-and-now reality. Hence, these things all hang together: the spiritual quest, meditative practice, and the spirit's requirement of honesty.

Acting Responsibly

Fourth, insofar as the human spirit moves us into reality, the spirit's concern is not only accurate knowledge but also proper action. So another spiritual requirement is that we be good-willed, loving, and responsible in our choices. This requirement means simply that our actions square with what we know—that we walk our talk, so to speak.

Yet knowledge alone does not determine actions. Sometimes many legitimate decisions may follow from the same fact. For example, knowing that the chance of rain is 80 percent does not tell us what to do about a long-planned picnic: cancel it, reschedule it, find an indoor facility, set up a tent, ask everyone to bring an umbrella, or simply take one's chances. So, in addition to acting in accord with the available knowledge, a further consideration plays into responsible and loving behavior: among the options that square with your knowledge, choose the option that best keeps the open-ended movement flowing.

It is not easy to state in any general way what makes for responsible behavior. I have proposed two criteria: act on the basis of the known facts and act in such as way as to keep positive growth flowing. Some would say simply, "Do the loving thing." A similar phrase is "Do the right thing." A traditional formula is "Do good and avoid evil." What these formulas mean in any particular case always remains to be seen. The decision comes down to us.

Whether or not we will "do the right thing" or "act lovingly" is up to us in spite of the fact that it may not always be easy to say exactly what is the right thing or the loving way. What is important is that we be committed to the right and the good and that we struggle to determine it and do it. This very commitment, however it might be phrased, is the fourth requirement of the human spirit and the fourth prerequisite of spiritual growth.

In this final case, perhaps more than in the other three, it is clear why these requirements are built-in: violation of them shuts down the whole system; growth stops; advance is halted; roadblocks are set up; the open-ended dynamism of the human spirit is restricted. Close-mindedness eventually leads to a dead end. Silliness and foolishness eventually exact a price. Dishonesty eventually catches up with us. Ill will or evil eventually self-destructs. Ah, here is one meaning of the too oft repeated and rote advice of the spiritual director from my seminary days: the spiritual life must be built on a solid foundation.

Thus, there are four basic requirements of the human spirit: that we be open, questioning, honest, and goodwilled. These four requirements correspond to the four-fold structure of the spirit—its capacity for experience, understanding, judgment, and decision. These four interact; they influence one another. Our decisions will determine what experience we will have. Our experience will affect the scope of our understanding. Our understanding and judgments will limit or expand our decisions. And so on, da capo. Therefore, these four are really varied expressions of one complex force, the dynamic human spirit within us acting in different ways at different times. The outgoing movement of the human spirit is the fundamental indicator of ethics or morality. To keep this movement flowing is the fundamental meaning of doing good.

When the spirit is functioning as it ought, when all its interacting dimensions are in synch, the spirit moves us on a path of open-ended unfolding. Some might want to name God as the end point of that path. Some would claim that God determines ethics. I continue to insist that such appeal to God is all too simple. The next chapter treats this matter of growth in the spirit more fully and brings the discussion to a close.

CHAPTER 20

Entering into the Flow
of the Universe

⌒⌒

W HAT A DELIGHT to see children at play! Sometimes
they get so excited that they prance about, dance in
circles, wave their arms, and beam all over. The joy of life shows
in their whole being. They cannot contain themselves. The
energy of the cosmos seems to be bubbling up through them.
And, in fact, it is. The human spirit within them, the leading
edge of evolutionary advance, is the source of their glee. They
are so sensitive to the spirit that they erupt with unbounded
wonder at all that the universe holds. Since they are still
unformed, still in the making, their spirits respond without
restriction. Of course, their response is sometimes inappropri-
ate. Children respond indiscriminately. At times their naïve
innocence is their beauty; at other times this very spontaneity is
their weakness. They are still immature. Their spiritual openness still needs to be channeled. On the other hand, the same
spirit that is in children is also in all of us, but growing up often
stamps it down. So, unfortunately, on the other extreme adults
are often dull, boring, and humdrum. They have lost their zest
for living. The challenge of the spiritual life is to get the child
and the adult together. The challenge is to recover the delight of
the child in the stability of the adult.

The human spirit is a wondrous openness to all that there is to be known and loved. The integration of that spirit into our very being is the essence of spiritual growth. This integration gears us, in turn, ever more surely toward an embrace of the universe. But to achieve that embrace, the human spirit must be functioning properly. Infantile haphazardness will not take us very far. The very nature of the spirit requires that it operate in a particular way. Only an open person will experience what there is; only a questioning person will come upon new ideas; only an honest person will ever discern the truth; and only a responsible and loving person will discover what ought to be done. The very makeup of the spirit includes built-in requirements for its effective functioning. In tune with our spirit, attentive to how it operates, we can formulate those requirements. We can discern the very laws of the human spirit. As we discussed, they are four: be open, questioning, honest, and loving.

The Four Laws

Those four laws derive from Bernard Lonergan's analysis of human consciousness or spirit. He himself phrased them in more technical terms: Be attentive, Be intelligent, Be reasonable, Be responsible. And he called them "the transcendental precepts." They are transcendental in that they apply to everything a person does; they are valid across the board. And they are absolutely general. They do not prescribe any particular behavior; they do not indicate *what* to do. Rather, they require a particular way of being; they indicate *how* we are to do whatever we do: attentively, intelligently, reasonably, and responsibly.

Lonergan also explained why there are four, where they come from, and how they interact with one another. You might notice, for example, that the first three have to do with knowledge—Be attentive: collect the data; Be intelligent: come up with some understanding; Be reasonable: base your judgment on the evidence, that is, check your understanding against the data to be sure your understanding is correct. These three parallel the steps in the textbook account of the scientific method: observation, hypothesis, and verification. And the fourth of the transcendental precepts has to do with actions—Be responsible: do what is right, good, loving. So, in a shorthand formula, you could reduce these four to two issues: correct understanding and correct doing. Said otherwise and with emphasis on the positive, the two concerns are knowledge and love. Emphasizing the same two aspects of the human spirit, philosophers have long spoken of intellect and will. And with a similar emphasis, religions are concerned about beliefs and morals—what one holds to be true and how one acts. Knowledge and love, intellect and will, beliefs and morals, these are all parallel indicators of the basic structure of the human spirit.

The Universality of Ethics

We tend to recognize the spiritual more easily when it appears in religious garb. So that final reference to religion—beliefs and morals—confirms that what I am talking about here is truly spiritual. I make those other technical connections—with science and philosophy—to suggest that what I am talking about is nothing novel or unknown but is a standard aspect of very widespread thinking. I introduced Lonergan's technical term *transcendental precepts* to emphasize again that the requirements of the human spirit are built-in; they are part and parcel of human nature; therefore, they apply wherever there are human beings. They are universal requirements. They apply to every human being regardless of era or nation or culture. For this reason they show up in so many different contexts and under so many different guises.

It is not important here to pursue all those technicalities. The important thing is my overall point: the requirements for ongoing human growth are built into our very beings. We know these requirements—there is no mystery about them, and we deceive ourselves to argue otherwise. We can implement them if we choose. We can also cast them aside and reject them.

Ethics—the determination of the right and wrong of behaviors—is built right into our human makeup. Ethics is not something that comes down from God in heaven by way of revelation. Ethics is not proper to religion. Ethics is a universal human thing, whether associated with religion or not. Confucius and Aristotle both proposed ethical systems that were not theological. But as human, neither is ethics something dependent on particular cultures. Yes, cultures have their customs, conventions, and traditions; but these things are not ethical; they are cultural, and there is a difference. Taboo is not the same as wrong; custom is not the same as ethics. There is nothing inherently correct about the American practice of driving on the right side of the road; there is nothing inherently wrong with women's wearing pants. Convention is not morality. And neither does ethics depend on each person's individual inclinations or sensitivities or whim. Ethics is not a subjective thing that changes as personal tastes and individual needs change. Lying to a prospective romantic partner does not become right just because I firmly believe it's part of the game, nor is it wrong for you only because you think it's wrong—although, in any case, to do what you believe to be wrong is surely the essence of personal corruption. Ethics is a universal requirement built into the structure of the human spirit.

The criteria of human life and growth are built into us human beings. To be an ethical or moral person does not mean to submit to some external authority—be it God and religion; society and culture; parents, family, and upbringing; or one's personal propensities. Ethics is not a matter of sacrificing one's freedom to outside forces; it is a matter of enhancing one's freedom by moving ever more surely along a path of open-ended unfolding. To be an ethical person means to be truly oneself, to

---

Ethics is not proper to religion. Ethics is a universal human thing, whether associated with religion or not.

---

be true to one's spiritual self, to assent to one's own capacity for open-ended growth. For this reason Lonergan speaks of obedience to the transcendental precepts as *authenticity*. One is authentic, one is a genuine human being, to the extent that one is open, questioning, honest, and loving. Otherwise, one dehumanizes oneself; one becomes less than human. The drug addict is again the glaring example of someone who insists on the right to exercise free choice and ends up with no freedom at all, a mere shell of a person. Ethics depends on following the requirements of human growth and development that are built into us as part of our spiritual nature. The human spirit itself is the ultimate source of ethics.

Ethics and God

One could also rightly say that ethics comes from God—but only insofar as "God" is the Creator of all things, including our own human spirits, and insofar as "God" set up the universe to function effectively in particular ways. Being ethical is merely discovering and following the ways of functioning that God built into the universe. Therefore, our immediate contact with ethics is in our own beings and in our interaction with the created universe. Contact with God, who is at work in the universe, is always secondary. Such contact depends on a go-between; it comes through our human spirits and is, therefore, indirect. So God is not the primary consideration when ethics or morals are at stake. Put God in or take God out and ethics remains the same. In fact, it is better to leave God out. When people begin appealing to God to legitimate their morality, they usually end up confusing things—as well as becoming dictatorial. Current debate over sexuality, abortion, stem-cell research, global warming, and cloning offer ready examples.

Nonetheless, the ethical person can be said to be on a godward path. He or she is working along the lines designed by the Creator for the ongoing unfolding of the creation. The ethical person freely enters the flow of the universe and by his or her deliberate choices contributes to that flow. The openness, questioning, honesty, and goodwill of the ethical person are the very qualities that foster positive unfolding. So, by embodying these qualities, the ethical person moves with the cosmic flow that unfolds in ever-broader being. Resonating with the plan of the Creator, in synch with the movement of the ages, attuned to the music of the stars, entering the flow of the universe, the ethical person moves along the path of spiritual and cosmic unfolding.

Ethics and Meditation

Two points bring home this discussion of ethics. First, meditation enhances one's spiritual sensitivities, so regular meditation inserts a person ever more deeply into the unfolding flow of the universe. For this reason deeply spiritual people are said to be powerful. The Jedi in the *Star Wars* series can control other people's thoughts. Similar claims—whether literally true or not, but always instructive—are made about saints and gurus throughout the ages. Spiritual adepts are powerful because they are profoundly in synch with the ultimate, overall flow of things. Rather than working against the flow, they are moving with it. Hence, they get farther.

I call this understanding the Bumper Car Model of cosmic unfolding. Like the amusement park ride that has people in cumbersome cars moving counterclockwise around a rink, so we are all moving through history. Sometimes some cars get out of line or even end up going backward. But these out-of-line cars cannot continue their devious path very long. Other cars moving with the flow will bump the deviants back in line, and the overall flow inevitably carries the day. Not always efficiently, but inevitably, the cars make their way around the rink. It is inconceivable that all the cars could somehow succeed in driving in the wrong direction.

The lesson in that model is that good will eventually win out. It is structured into the universe; it defines the meaning of unfolding; and it ultimately determines the flow of things. Counterforces will inevitably be reversed. They are but regrettable aberrations in an already determined process. People committed to the good, people who are spiritually attuned, participate in the ultimate power—because the principles of the unfolding of goodness that are built into the universe are the very principles that structure our human spirits. Therefore, insofar as meditation purifies our human spirits, it attunes us ever more clearly to the growth-producing forces of the universe.

Second, this discussion of ethics makes clear why all the spiritual traditions emphasize good living. Part and parcel of spiritual growth is ethical behavior. The ongoing integration of the human spirit into the permanent structures of the psyche results in a person who is ever more ethical. Ethics and spirituality are two sides of the same coin.

To me this point seems glaringly obvious, yet it needs to be emphasized. Some recent "spiritual" thinking denies the importance, and the very validity, of ethics. Still confusing ethics with custom, taboo, and cultural tradition, this thinking claims that spiritually developed people move beyond concern for ethics. They just act as they wish.

This topic is subtle. Certainly, some of the things individual persons and whole religions put forth as ethical requirements are nonsense—like the restricted role of women, the evils of nonprocreative sex, the wickedness of modern medical procedures, the unquestioned right of the wealthy to their privileged way of life, the military defense of national prerogatives "for God and country." So if someone disagrees with the supposed moral teaching about these things and says that he or she is "beyond ethical concerns," has this person really moved beyond ethics or just beyond ethical nonsense? Abraham Maslow pointed out that self-actualizing people—that is, highly integrated people—are exceedingly ethical yet they often ignore the rules of expected behavior. It is not that spiritual growth moves one beyond ethics. Rather, spiritual growth makes one profoundly ethical and, therefore, sometimes out of synch with superficial, conventional "ethics." Profoundly spiritual people "just act as they wish" because they only wish to act as one ought. They are living out the ethics built into their very beings. They are simply following Saint Augustine's rule, "Love, and do what you will."

The Enduring Importance of Ethics

There is a further consideration. Within a profound spiritual experience itself, there is, indeed, no concern for ethics. There is no concern for anything. There is no this or that, no here or there, no yes or no; there is just pure presence. Any concern whatever would be a drifting of the mind. To think about ethical matters, or anything else, during the moment of intense self-transcendence is impossible. To this extent, it can be said that ethics is not a part of the spiritual realm.

However, this fact does not mean that the self-transcendence itself is an ethically neutral matter. In fact, the experience is transcendent precisely because it is moving along the lines of unfolding that are built into the universe and into the human spirit. One could say that a purely spiritual experience is precisely an experience of the very movement of ethics through the universe.

Of course, with Platonic philosophy, Gnosticism, most Eastern philosophy, and New Age religion, some believe that the spiritual realm is the really real and that this earthly existence is a passing illusion. They would insist, then, that the spiritual experience is the measure of all things. Thus, they conclude that ethics—and all thinking!—is irrelevant. This conclusion is surely misguided. Derived from the supposed spiritual realm, it dictates procedures in the supposed earthly realm. It depends on a false separation of the physical and the spiritual—that dualism again!—and then it relies on an illicit remixing of the two supposed realms. At stake is the same self-contradiction that I noted before in such matters: the claim to derive truth-claims from a realm in which truth-claims are said to be irrelevant. A balanced understanding of these matters can sort the whole thing out, as I have been doing here.

The considered claim that ethics has no part with advanced spirituality is charlatanism. All the spiritual traditions include guidelines for proper living. Ethics and spirituality involve one another.

God In and Out of the Picture

Finally, there is also God. For those who wish, God easily fits into the spiritual and ethical picture that I have been drawing.

In fact, for most people, talk of God is not really about the Creator-God of the Universe, the Great Mystery, the Known Unknown Behind All Things. God-talk is usually a shorthand way of talking about good human living—ethics or morality. Indeed, using that shorthand, I could have made my points in these last two chapters much more easily. Of course, I would have contributed no understanding to these matters: I would have merely reinforced the simplistic notion that ethics and religion go together. I would also have left out all unbelievers. I would also have necessarily had to choose one particular religious view to push, and then I would have had to leave out some believers, as well. So I chose not to speak of God at all but, rather, of our unfolding spiritual nature and its synchronization with the universe, even though, for those who wish, God can easily fit into this picture.

But for anyone uncomfortable with easy talk of God, God can also be left out of this picture—and nothing changes. Nothing changes, I submit, because the very requirements for wholesome human living, which are attributed to "God," are actually built into the universe and into us. So any knowledge we have of these requirements derives initially from the human spirit itself. And to it, theists and nontheists alike have equal access.

I used to think that the spiritual quest had to do with closeness to God and possible visions, revelations, and divine consolations, though no one in my theological training seemed to know very much about such things. Now I understand that no one knew about those things because, for the most part, they are false issues. From a theological perspective, they are nothing to know about. They are matters of psychology and sometimes of psychopathology.

First and foremost, the spiritual quest is about integrating the human spirit into the structures of the personality. Meditation is a powerful tool for effecting this integration. By its very nature, spiritual integration brings with it ethical living as well as broader awareness and deeper experience overall. When these notions are understood, those who want to turn this discussion in a theological direction could accurately say that spiritual integration also brings closeness with God. But this theological turn is optional.

Over the years I have come to understand these things. Spiritually, I have grown up. I have moved beyond childish ways. My hard-won understanding has taken me to a whole new place. These spiritual matters hardly seem to be what I was grappling with as an idealistic youth. Yet, from another point of view, I realize that I have actually come to what I was seeking, and, finding it, I recognize it. In my current spiritual pursuits, unorthodox as they might seem, I am actually touching that deep mystery that fascinated, enticed, and drew me on from the beginning. In ways that I could never have imagined then, I am now truly pursuing the spiritual ideal that I once described as "being a holy priest."

I hope my life's learning will help you, my reader, as well, to recover the delight of your childhood and the idealism of your own youth. I hope you will find ways to retain that delight and to live out that idealism as a contributing adult in the sophisticated, multifaceted, and wondrous world of the twenty-first century.

Of Related Interest

———■———

Thomas Keating

INTIMACY WITH GOD
An Introduction to Centering Prayer

"For all those aspiring to a genuine spiritual life, Father Keating has charted a course that will take us progressively closer to our divine goal as we learn to touch God, first with the words of our lips, then with reflections of the mind and with the feelings of the heart."

—Living Prayer

"Multifarious are the books on prayer and spirituality. Now and then, one sparkles. . . . This is such a book."

—Praying

"This is perhaps Keating's most readable and enlightening work. Filled with insight and practical advice, it offers sound wisdom on the way that centering prayer can deepen our intimacy with God."

—Spiritual Book News

Centering prayer—you've heard about it, now learn how to do it. Keating, a Trappist monk and former abbot, teaches us this method of nonvocal prayer based on the desert fathers and mothers and the work of St. John of the Cross.

0-8245-1588-9, $16.95 paperback

———■———

crossroad

Of Related Interest

RICHARD ROHR

EVERYTHING BELONGS
The Gift of Contemplative Prayer

Revised & Udated!

Richard Rohr has written this book to help us pray
better and see life differently. Using parables, koans,
and personal experiences, he leads us beyond the
techniques of prayer to a place where we can receive
the gift of contemplation: the place where (if only for
a moment) we see the world in God clearly, and
know that everything belongs.

0-8245-2278-8, $17.95 paperback

---

crossroad

Of Related Interest